Best Wishes,

Joe Black

What People Are Saying . . .

This book is a "must read." It focuses on a critical issue of the '90s—Balancing quality in the work place with quality in your life. I got lots of good ideas from it. Very readable.

Robert J. Kriegel, Ph.D.
author of *If It Ain't Broke . . . Break It!*

With his unique blend of humor, warmth and insight, Joe Black offers easy-to-implement suggestions for anyone seeking to improve his or her quality of life. *Looking Back On The Future* is brimming with ideas—some straightforward, some subtle—that can help you sort out the priorities of life. This is a book you'll come back to again and again.

Douglas L. Donivan
Vice President, Operations
Liberty Insurance Services

This book is a "spiritual gift" and a wonderful crosscheck to ensure personal and organizational values are in sync. It is full of *wisdom* and provides many opportunities to make each day more rewarding!

Chap Johnston
COO
Tanner Companies, Inc.

Joe Black was deeply involved in a change of management philosophy and style which led a Malcolm Baldrige National Quality Award-winning company to spectacular improvements in productivity and morale of the associates within that company. This experience, as well as that gleaned from his consulting company, EQM, provides him insights which he is able to share with his readers in this book.

Joab M. Lesesne, Jr.
President
Wofford College

Joe Black has again brought the lessons of quality to everyday application in a person's life. Truly, what happens around the kitchen table is as important as what happens around the board room table, and *Looking Back On The Future* so clearly focuses on the big Q for all of us. It is a book for all people, for daily living.

Olin H. Broadway, Jr.
Chairman
Heron, Inc.

Joe Black's second book reflects all of the upbeat, positive, quality-oriented attitudes that shine through in his personal style as a speaker, a business leader, and a friend. His vignettes, interspersed with "quotable quotes," give the reader inspirational material for personal reflection and practical application. Any business person interested in the continuous improvement process will enjoy discovering the parallels Joe draws between quality in the workplace and quality in one's personal life.

Susan A. Hodge
Assistant Vice President
Corporate Banking
New York Branch
Dresdner Bank

Readers of Joe Black's books will come to a realization early on that his basic message—it's out there for all who practice what he preaches—will overpower whatever obstacles may appear. His infectious zeal is the kind that will uplift all who subscribe to it.

> Gibson Gayle, Jr.
> Lawyer
> Houston, Texas

I found a lot to relate to and reflect upon in Joe's latest book. It offers much food for thought on our interpersonal relationships on all levels of our personal and professional lives.

> William H. Hill, M.D.
> Spartanburg, South Carolina

Looking Back On The Future is great and easy reading.

> Louis P. Batson, Jr.
> Chairman
> Louis P. Batson Company

Sharing lessons learned from "down home truths," Joe Black takes the mystery out of achieving continuous improvement. His conviction that common sense values and ethics prepare us to meet life's challenges outshines the complex and the complicated. Joe's book is a dazzling reminder that mankind is enriched through faithfulness to steadfast principles!

> Jack Enen
> President
> The Enen Group

Looking Back On the Future
Building a Quality Foundation

by

JOE BLACK

LIFE VISION BOOKS
P.O. Box 98
Campobello, SC 29322

The following trademarks appear throughout this book: Weed Eater, Magic Marker.

First printing 1993

ISBN 0-9628474-3-7
LCCN 92-74329

Editing, design, typesetting, and printing services provided by About Books, Inc., 425 Cedar Street, Buena Vista, CO 81211, 800-548-1876.

ATTENTION CORPORATIONS, COLLEGES, AND PRO-FESSIONAL ORGANIZATIONS: Quantity discounts are available on bulk purchases of this book for educational purposes or fund raising. Special books or book excerpts can also be created to fit specific needs. For information, please contact Life Vision Books, P.O. Box 98, Campobello, SC 29322 or call 800-348-9953.

Dedication

This book is dedicated to my wife
and greatest supporter, Kathy.

Acknowledgments

This book was written in hotel rooms, on airplanes, and in the wee hours of the morning in my home study before the work day began. There is time to do what we want to do!

I wish to express appreciation to my wife, Katherine Virginia Beeks Black, and to her parents, Jennie and Norman, for their support and encouragement over the years.

A special thanks goes to my mother, Frederica, and my father, Bill, for without their love and support and their belief in me, there would have been no foundation on which to build.

Thanks as well to all my teammates at EQM, the finest folks I've ever had the pleasure of working with.

A sincere thanks too for the invaluable help with this book from Tom and Marilyn Ross of About Books in Buena Vista, Colorado.

Preface

I guess I hear the question at least once per week, "How do you do it?" or the statement, "I don't see how you get it all done!" My answer is always the same: One Step at a Time.

I am 35 years old at this writing; currently Vice President of Customer Services for Duke Power Company; a wife to husband, Bob; and mother to Rob, Matthew, and Abby, ages seven, three, and one, respectively. We have already raised our nephew David, now age 23 and recently married. Wow! It makes me tired when I think about it, and that's just the point—I don't focus on the magnitude! I try to focus on each bite-sized piece: each major project at work, each goal for my children, each date with my husband, each "opportunity" in the workplace, each peanut butter fingerprint on my skirt-tail. . .

How can I do it when there is simply so much to deal with?! Read *Looking Back On The Future* and learn some secrets of maintaining a Quality life, not just a focus on quality at work *or* just quality in the workplace but QUALITY as a way of life.

It all begins with building a QUALITY foundation. Joe will so beautifully remind you in his conversational style that Quality begins with setting some priorities, determining what's important to you, focusing on those priorities and living them out in your life—one step, one relationship, one action at a time.

I am very fortunate to have had a strong QUALITY foundation even from my earliest days. My family has played a vital role, as has Joe's, in the development of my very basic values and priorities. My Dad taught me years ago that priorities are basic to happiness in this life. We used to go through a little exercise where he would ask, "Who's first, who's second . . . ?" The older I get, the wiser this has become in my eyes. At a very early age he motivated me to begin to focus on the things that are important to me.

I would answer these questions today very simply: 1) God, 2) Myself (not in a selfish way but being sure I am making the most of my skills, talents, and abilities, and being sure that I continue to grow spiritually and mentally and stay strong physically and emotionally), 3) my husband, 4) my children, 5) my extended family and friends, and 6) my work and work associates. These priorities are my foundation—they are what counts.

Is it always easy to keep them in order? —Absolutely Not!

Do I often lose my balance? —Yes Sir!

Does it all work perfectly? —No Way!

Are there days I want to hide in the closet and hope it goes away? —Yes Sireee!

Is my life one of joy? —YES!

Would I make any significant changes? —NO

Do I have it all? —No Way!

Life is a series of choices: some are tough, some are easy, some are important, some are trivial. But whatever their type, happiness comes when I'm focused on my priorities—the foundation that makes me the person I am.

Life is such a wonderful gift. I have heard my Mom say it so often, "God gives us one light, one life . . . let it shine!" As you read this book and look back on *your* future, consider how bright your light is shining. You are bound to get a few new sparks with each page you read!

You will enjoy this book. You'll laugh. You may cry. But you are certain to look within yourself. Are you living on a QUALITY foundation?

Through Joe's own journey, you will identify some ways you can firm your foundation, no matter how unstable it may seem today.

Read and enjoy . . .

Sharon Allred Decker
Vice President, Customer Services
Duke Power Company

Contents

Foreword

Joe Black and I have known each other as both business associates and friends for several years now. My wife, Nell, and I visit Joe and his wife, Kathy, from time to time and always leave a little better for the experience. Joe has an often-quoted saying that "attitudes are contagious!" Theirs are definitely worth "catching." What makes this book so special is that Joe Black hasn't simply written it—he's lived it!

Joe has a fine appreciation for the value of balance in living and balance in doing. He explains to his readers that to be fit for life, one needs a balance of the physical, mental, and spiritual sides of our being.

This book clearly defines positive, creative energy. The reader understands that positive, creative energy flows best through integrated circuits that run throughout all areas of our lives. It starts with the family, and Joe's wise observation that "the quality of what goes on around your family's kitchen table is far more important than the quality of what goes on around your board room table" hits at the heart of the matter.

The well-lived life is one of continuous discovery and learning. Humor and a positive mental attitude are essential companions along the way. This book is for the person who is serious about finding new perspectives from which to see wonder in life. It is a joy to read and an inspiration for living.

Charles E. "Gus" Whalen, Jr.
President and Chief Executive Officer
The Warren Featherbone Company

Introduction

In today's fast-paced world, it is essential we understand the importance of balancing quality in our personal and professional lives. If we choose to trade one for the other, we're likely to have only bittersweet victories.

Looking Back On the Future is a different book. This collection of vignettes is my attempt to correlate the quality of personal life with that of professional life. In truth, the two cannot be separated. In an effort to convey the strong influence of childhood infrastructure on our later lives, I share with you not only my experiences as a professional in the business world, but also several lessons gleaned from looking back to my preteen and adolescent days. I firmly believe the most effective leaders I've encountered built their careers on strong family foundations.

The last decade's focus on *total quality* in the workplace must now make way for an emphasis on *continuous improvement* in every aspect of our lives. Finally let's understand continuous improvement is more than a process—it's a way of life!

We're Thinking 80% Waste

Did you know 80% of the thinking time spent by American adults dwells on either anger about the past or worry about the future? This amazing statistic was published by a respected national psychiatric association in 1991. Think about that. Eighty percent of most adults' thinking time focuses on the past—which is gone forever—or is spent worrying about the future, which may never come. What a waste.

When I first read this fact, I couldn't believe it. However, as I've reflected on it more, it is not so inconceivable. Just listen to people's conversations. Watch television or listen to the radio. Read newspapers and magazines. True, isn't it? Just 20% of our time is focused on the only time any of us actually have—the present.

Think of what we could do if we reversed the percentages: 20% on the past and future and 80% on *the now*. I'll bet if you and I focus 80% of our thinking time on the present and consciously live each day as if it were our last, the future will miraculously take care of itself. We can and should learn from the past—but we shouldn't live in it.

The Precious Present is a wonderful book by Dr. Spencer Johnson in which he discloses a simple secret: the present is all we have and it can be wonderful if we decide we want it to be.

The cynics of our world will never understand. So what? The important thing is *we* do. Remember—don't be angry about the past—you can't change one thing. Neither will the course of your future be altered by worry.

Focus on doing the right and best things in the present. If you do, you will give yourself the best gift of all—the precious present!

JUST NOTES

_____

_____

_____

_____

_____

_____

_____

_____

"We become what we think."

Anonymous

_____

_____

_____

_____

_____

_____

_____

_____

_____

_____

_____

_____

_____

_____

Matthew, Mark, Luke, and My Sandbox

I was nine years old. It was blue-sky and open-mind time in my back yard. Another sunny Sunday of watching marshmallow clouds billowing across the endless sapphire sky. In my large sandbox, I was busy reaching far past the dry sand of the surface, deep into the pile where moist grains met my fingertips. The tunnels would serve well for my toy trucks and train to pass through. The mimosa tree blew in the breeze as I reveled in a world known only to little boys in their own *magic kingdom*.

My playing was interrupted by my mother calling, "Joe." Again, "Joe," as she climbed the hill to my imaginary mountain top. "Are you ready for tonight?"

"Yes, Mother," I assured, "I'm ready."

"Joe, are you sure you're ready?"

"Yes, Mother. I am sure," I asserted, continuing to smooth the edges around my perfectly constructed sand tunnels.

As evening approached, I thought of the conversation with my mother and began to recognize the challenge facing me that night. What was I going to do? I knew I wasn't ready to recite the books of the New Testament to the entire First Baptist Church of Pickens, South Carolina. What on earth was I thinking when I told my mother I was ready? The joy I'd experienced in my sandpile had pushed out any serious thoughts.

As I bathed, dressed, and combed my hair, panic set in. What would I do? I'd never get past Matthew, Mark, Luke, and John! What would my father, a deacon in the church, say? Would my parents laugh, cry, give me a spanking, or worse? Maybe no one will come to church, I hoped. Or maybe the crowd will be so small they will cancel the service.

As we drove to church in our 1952 Chevrolet, I could feel my hands sweating. Mother looked at me, smiled, patted me on the head, and called me a good boy. Oh, no—cars were already in the parking lot when we pulled up. People had come.

Once inside, I realized the church was packed. It seemed everyone in Pickens County had come to see me mess up. As the service started, I looked at the bulletin in my hand. After the hymn, I would be up.

I stood slowly, walked to the front of the church, and turned to face the masses. Smiling, I opened my mouth, "I will now recite the books of the New Testament: January, February, March, April, May, June, July, August, September, October, November, December." Smiling once again, I sat down.

What had I done? What did God think? What did Mother and Dad think? I was disgraced! I stared at the floor. I thought I heard adult laughter outside the church, but I knew in my humiliation I was just hearing things.

Somehow I survived that Sunday night ordeal. Years later, my father told me he and the other deacons who occupied the back pew as ushers had left the church that night after my recitation—splitting their sides with laughter. I hadn't imagined the laughter after all. For some time after my performance, I was known as the "Calendar Boy" in our church.

I don't know what I learned from this experience other than it pays to think on your feet. At least I showed the crowd I knew something! My parents made sure I learned the books of not only the New Testament, but the Old Testament as well—all of which I recited to the congregation the next Sunday night.

Memories of those days linger in my mind. My sandpiles and toys have taken different forms as I've grown older. I still play with them with one exception . . . I do my homework first! We can't get by with being *calendar boys* in the adult world when we haven't done our homework.

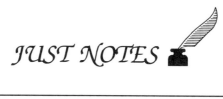

JUST NOTES

_____

_____

_____

_____

_____

_____

_____

_____

"Anything worth doing is worth doing poorly, until you can learn to do it well."

Steve Brown

_____

_____

_____

_____

_____

_____

_____

_____

_____

_____

_____

_____

_____

Put Your Heart Into It

What does it take to "make it" in life—to be a success, accomplish meaningful things, and leave our world a little better place? For centuries, humankind has pondered such questions. You can read biographies of famous and not-so-famous people and discover there are almost as many ways to succeed in life as there are people. Is it fate, luck, or happenstance that leads some to especially enjoyable or meaningful experiences in life? Does anyone really know?

Writers, philosophers, and scholars reflect and debate constantly on what constitutes success. Those in the business community draw parallels from their own experiences and hold themselves up as examples of how to accomplish ambitions and goals. Mega-egos often drive these *enlightened* few.

It has been my experience that most people actually don't believe they can control their destinies. Instead they feel luck plays a major role in their successes or failures. To hold this belief is tragic.

You and I *do* control our lives almost totally. But only if we are inspired, focused on life's opportunities, and determined to follow our dreams. To live in such a way requires more than motivation; it requires inspiration. To be inspired is to reach a state far beyond motivation. Inspiration requires us to define and understand our purpose in life. Defining your purpose in life is quite different from setting and attaining goals.

I overheard an interesting conversation while waiting in the Charlotte airport. Seated next to me were two gentlemen, each trying to impress the other with tales of accomplishment. One man made a comment more profound than he may have realized. He said of his young son, "My boy is a good football player with great potential, but he's gotten to the stage where if his heart's not in it, he may get hurt."

As I began to think about that, I realized it is true in life as well as in football. If we work hard, prepare for life's daily challenges, and put our hearts into whatever we do, we're all more likely to experience success.

Putting our hearts into our endeavors doesn't mean we won't get hurt—but it has everything to do with succeeding in life. I recently read that a successful person goes from one failure to the next enthusiastically! If we play the game of life with inspired hearts and heads, we're likely to have fewer failures and be able to cope with them positively when they do occur.

Think about your personal and professional life. If you're like me, most of your hurts result from your own decisions. Most people refuse to accept their failures because it's easier to blame someone or something else. We all need to recognize that if our heart's not in *it* (you define the *it*), we are likely to fail. Successful people put their hearts—and their heads—into whatever they do!

JUST NOTES

_____
_____
_____
_____
_____
_____
_____
_____
_____

"Strong lives are motivated by dynamic purposes."

Anonymous

_____
_____
_____
_____
_____
_____
_____
_____
_____
_____
_____
_____
_____
_____
_____
_____

Good Teachers

At 5:00 A.M. I stopped at a Waffle House Restaurant on South Carolina Interstate 85. A "Good Morning" from the waitress greeted me as I entered. Taking my seat on a stool at the bar, I noticed I was the only customer other than an old gentleman who sat down beside me.

The waitress knew him, "Hello, Sam. Good to see you again. Where have you been?"

"With my sister," he answered. "She's got a nice place and lets me sleep on her couch. She's got one of them new mobile homes. They don't call 'em trailers now, you know. Yeah, it really is nice. Nobody bothers me at my sister's."

I ordered my breakfast and the waitress said, "Sam, do you want to sweep the parking lot this morning before the crowd gets here?"

"Yeah," he replied, and walked to a closet door, opened it, and picked up a broom and trash can. Out the door he went and began sweeping the lot in the cold February wind.

I was drinking my coffee when the waitress said, "Look at Sam out there. He's a good man, but somewhat retarded (a word rarely heard today). He always wants to completely sweep our parking lot before he'll eat. He says he wants to work for his breakfast. He has no money."

The next thing I knew, the door opened and Sam said to me, "Mister, will you move your car? The wind blew some trash under it and I can't get to it."

I was warm—enjoying my pancakes and bacon—but when the waitress looked at me with a twinkle in her eye, I knew the proper response to Sam's request. "Yes sir," I replied.

I returned to my breakfast after moving my car. Fifteen minutes passed and I was about to leave when Sam returned.

His breakfast was waiting—he sat down and looked at me, "Do you work, mister?"

I responded in the affirmative.

"I work here once or twice a month," he continued. "I usually work on the Wal-Mart lot—that's a big one—takes me a good week to finish it. Yep, that's a big job alright."

"Really?" I answered. "I often shop at Wal-Mart and wondered who swept that lot. It's always so clean. You do a great job." Sam beamed. The waitress smiled at me, winked, and mouthed a "thank you."

I stood up, left a tip, wished Sam and the waitress a good day, and left. I had wanted to get an early start on my day, hopefully to work out a problem that had popped up the day before. Now somehow it was more like an opportunity than a problem.

All during that day, I kept thinking of Sam. I made sure I moved the cars so I could do a very thorough job on the parking lots I swept that day. Funny how we can learn from really good teachers!

JUST NOTES

_____

_____

_____

_____

_____

_____

_____

_____

"Many eyes go through the meadow, but few see the flowers in it."

Ralph Waldo Emerson

_____

_____

_____

_____

_____

_____

_____

_____

_____

_____

_____

_____

A Fifties Foundation

I grew up in the small town of Pickens, South Carolina. My childhood was not unlike that of Wally and The Beaver of the television series, "Leave it to Beaver." Although no television producers darkened our door, my parents, Bill and Frederica, my sister, Linda, and I would have been excellent subjects for such a sitcom.

Every morning at six, my dad rose to have breakfast and catch Dave Garroway and his chimp friend, Mugs, on the new NBC "Today Show." Then he'd crank up his 1952 Chevrolet and drive 20 miles to his job in Greenville, South Carolina.

There he spent the day doing whatever dads did in the '50s, then returned home promptly at five each afternoon. This routine remained constant for 42 years until he retired. My dad set a priceless example for my sister and me. Of course, he never realized his example was etching a good work ethic into his children. But because my father was so faithful to his job, I grew up thinking every adult male never missed a day of work come rain, snow, or shine.

My mother cajoled me out of bed each morning with crumbs of news bulletins from television. Even as a young boy, I had a keen interest in world events. My mother's bulletins varied from Khrushchev's activities, to "the bomb," to snow on the local weather forecast. These gentle news flashes served as an effective prod to get me out of bed. I'd get up, dress, eat breakfast, and get my schoolbooks together. Then my sister and I would wait for our neighbor, Mrs. Wallis, and her two girls to pick us up and drive us to school in their green, four-door Buick.

Linda, four years my senior, always emerged from her room in the morning beautiful and well groomed. Kindly tolerant of her rambunctious younger brother, she usually walked to Mrs. Wallis' Buick while I ran ahead. I enjoyed getting to the car first so I could hold the door open for her. I imagine she thought nervous energy propelled me to the car at such speed. In truth, it was my way of blazing the trail for her to make a graceful entrance.

Life seemed forever and time was endless in those wonder years. My hometown was the whole world to me. The quality of life I enjoyed was a 12 on a scale of 10! And I had sense enough *even then* to realize just how good it was. I am very thankful for that.

What a foundation from which to launch each new day! What a joy to scoop up life, swallow it whole, and not gain a pound. Every scoop was transformed into pure boyhood energy. My substructure was built on love in a real, yet make-believe world.

Linking those bygone days to the opportunities I have enjoyed as an adult has been a relatively smooth transition for me. Although I'm not sure why this is true, I believe it has everything to do with the unconditional love I received from my parents and others. I always had folks there to love and support me.

A strong foundation is so important to building a meaningful life. You may be laying the groundwork for someone without even being aware of it. In case you are, why not make sure a *quality* life is likely to be built upon it—a young life may depend on your skills and good example!

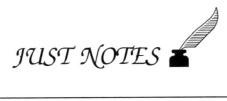

JUST NOTES

_____

_____

_____

_____

_____

_____

_____

_____

"As the twig is bent, so is the tree inclined."

Alexander Pope

_____

_____

_____

_____

_____

_____

_____

_____

_____

_____

_____

_____

_____

_____

_____

The Screamer

A young lady, recently hired by the hotel where my company was conducting a Continuous Improvement Seminar, pulled me aside and asked if she could talk with me. She told me she had been listening to my presentation on quality awareness for the past two days while she was preparing refreshments for our breaks. She wanted my opinion about a problem.

"What do you do when your boss is constantly screaming at you and cursing day in and day out? It's so unfair because no one has given me any training in how to do my job."

"What a sad but common problem," I thought. No one is born knowing how to do a job. He or she must be properly trained and educated as to the best way to accomplish their assigned tasks. Mistakes are usually caused for two reasons:

1. A lack of proper education/training. No one comes to work wanting to make mistakes or wanting to have a bad day.

2. Lack of attention or an "I don't care" attitude.

The second reason is often but not always closely related to the first. Both are typically due to management not focusing on, and investing in, the proper training for their associates.

This young lady was attractive, obviously intelligent, and she wanted to do her best. I asked if she had talked with her boss about the problem.

"No," she responded. "I'm afraid of him."

Wanting to know more about her, I inquired if she felt comfortable sharing a little of her background. Carolyn told me about her family, where she was from, her educational background, and work experience. Although she was a very smart person, she had not enjoyed many of the benefits you and I have received in life. Her self-confidence was low. Rather than blooming, she was wilting under her boss.

I explained no person has the *right* to yell or curse at another, that she was a unique human being and deserved respect. If she allowed people to treat her with disrespect, she would contend with it all her life. How others treated her was her decision to make, not theirs.

She looked as though a revelation had dawned. "I really never stopped to realize that this is true." She thanked me, said she appreciated my time, and went on her way.

Two days later, I was in my hotel room when the telephone rang. It was Carolyn. "Mr. Black, could you meet me in the lobby? I want to talk with you . . . I must talk with you."

I said I'd be right down. Several possible scenarios ran through my mind as the elevator whisked me down to the lobby.

There was Carolyn—all smiles. "Mr. Black, I've thought a lot about our conversation and I've read your book, *The Attitude Connection*." She continued, "I have just come from my boss' office. He began screaming at me again this afternoon and I asked him to sit down. To my surprise, he did, then I told him, 'Stop screaming at me; you're hurting me. Please stop.' To my amazement, he replied, 'Why didn't you tell me before? I scream at everyone who works for me until they tell me to stop.'" She assured me she would never again work for anyone who yelled at her.

"Carolyn, I'm proud of you. I hope things will be better between you and your boss now."

"Oh, he's not my boss anymore. I quit. After our conversation two days ago, I went to visit my friend at the Marriott Hotel. She's so happy there; she told me the Marriott folks all treat each other with respect. When I learned they had a position open, I applied. They hired me to start next week. I'm a smart person, Mr. Black. I don't have to take verbal abuse. I know that now." She thanked me and invited me to come to the Marriott to conduct our seminars next time we were in the area.

When she left, I felt like a million bucks! Isn't it amazing the positive influence we can have on other people's lives when we take the time to care?

Two events conclude this story:

1. The screaming boss stopped me the next day in the hall and said he understood I was the reason one of his best employees had left.

   "No, sir," I retorted as I walked off, "You're the reason!"

2. I moved our next seminar to the Marriott Hotel. They truly are a quality organization and they don't scream at their associates!

JUST NOTES

_____

_____

_____

_____

_____

_____

_____

_____

"What happens is not as important as how you react to what happens."

Thaddeus Golas

_____

_____

_____

_____

_____

_____

_____

_____

_____

_____

_____

_____

_____

Are You Married to Quality?

When a company truly wants to marry continuous improvement, it becomes necessary to design and implement a customized quality PROCESS, not just a generic PROGRAM. Since each company has a unique culture, customization is a requirement. Every associate must understand and believe in excellence. They need to understand *why* it is necessary to always do their jobs right. Associates at every level must strive to service their *internal* clients' wants and needs. Until this happens they can't possibly service the needs and wants of their external customers. Education is required to ensure the best improvement at all levels. The care ratio of all associates for one another must be raised. A feeling of ownership of the company's continuous improvement process by all associates is critical in this competitive world. Marketing, sales, administration, manufacturing, and customer service all must apply this quality attitude before an organization can achieve excellence.

A breakthrough in attitudes is key to meaningful breakthroughs in the quality of products and services. All associates need to examine their personal and professional goals in an orderly, forthright, self-discovery method. If you're *committed* to continuous improvement, this is worth every effort. If you are simply interested, it won't work for you.

When you take a hard look at your failure/error costs, the opportunities are mind-boggling! Huge breakthroughs are possible if leaders are committed to educating, implementing, setting the example, and letting go of some of the *power* they've held in the past. One key is to raise the quality awareness ratio of all associates and have the majority arrive at individual decisions to "buy in." Tremendous savings can be realized when an organization defines its own continuous-improvement process, but only when associates take ownership.

The question is simple: "Do you want to flirt with, court, become engaged to, or marry long-term quality and excellence?" The *Wall Street Journal* recently featured an article about leadership versus managing. It said, "You can *lead* a horse to water, but you cannot *manage* it to drink." Associates will drink deeply of quality and excellence when they understand how and why it is necessary. Quality is simple; people are complicated.

Recognizing the need to start and actually committing to build, educate, and follow up are decisions leaders must make if their companies are to be the best. Too few are willing to commit! Quality commitment is reflected in EVERYTHING a person does. It is a leader's responsibility to lead, not manage.

Are you in love with quality or just shacking up with it? A "that's close enough—ship it" mentality is not even being acquainted with continuous improvement . . . let alone married to it!

JUST NOTES

_____

_____

_____

_____

_____

_____

_____

_____

_____

"Marriage should, I think, always be a little hard and new and strange. It should be breaking your shell and going into another world and a bigger one."

Anne Morrow Lindbergh

_____

_____

_____

_____

_____

_____

_____

_____

_____

_____

_____

_____

_____

The Corporate Filter

Since the day Henry Ford's first Model-T rolled off the assembly line, Americans have had a passion for their automobiles. I remember my first car, a used 1960 Pontiac station wagon. I paid $600 for this tank which got about 11 miles to the gallon. I sat up nights proudly staring at it. I still enjoy my vehicles and try to take good care of them. A car these days costs more than I paid for my first house!

Maintaining any vehicle properly requires changing the engine's filters on a regular basis. The purpose, of course, is to keep out trash or impurities which could damage the engine. A good filter protects the engine so it can run effectively and efficiently.

Over 20 some years, I've observed a different type of filter. It usually doesn't help the engine at all. I am referring to the *corporate filter*. The corporate filter is comprised of managers—not leaders—who filter reality from their CEOs. These corporate filters are amazing. Layers of them surround most top executives in the United States. A lot of executives I've worked with seem to believe filters are necessary. Fear fuels corporate filters—fear of telling or hearing the truth.

Today's workworld has everybody stressed out. Stress levels could be greatly reduced if corporate filters were eliminated—from location to location, business unit to business unit, division to division, marketing to manufacturing, corporate to line. The engines driving America's industry would hum with renewed vigor if "the top" were bold enough to eliminate their filters.

In years of dealing with top level executives, nothing intrigues me more than these obvious filter systems. Most companies have filters; some are quite simple while others are large and bureaucratic. Some are *stealth filters*—you can rarely detect them. These can be deadly to a company.

How does a CEO avoid being cut off from vital data, facts, and realities which are so necessary to high caliber leadership? One sure way is to flatten the organization. That simply means removing one or more rows of filters—they usually add little value and often are paid—but don't earn—enormous salaries. The most effective leaders are the ones who avoid filters. These winners *make* time to spend with the people who actually do the work. And they not only hear their people, they also *listen*.

Every CEO I've worked with over the years has known about corporate filters. But few have chosen to do anything about them. Why? I often wonder if some really *want to* know what is happening in their operation. Perhaps some top execs enjoy having filters to screen out unpleasant truths. Of course opportunities are filtered out as well.

Putting the fear of God into employees guarantees a wonderful filter for the boss. Managers may feel filters reduce the stress levels accompanying their demanding jobs. Some may even rationalize they are delegating responsibility and growing their people. There are dozens of reasons to have filter systems—none of them very good.

The bottom line should be: if an executive doesn't want to lead without truth filters, he or she doesn't deserve the privilege of navigating the company ship. With filters, one day the ship will surely hit an iceberg and maybe even sink.

The workers of America deserve leaders, not managers with filters. They deserve top executives who care enough to *demand* the facts. They deserve leaders who won't strap on their golden parachutes and bail, leaving the people who are the backbone and soul of the company to crash and burn.

As a leader, do you enjoy a warm and fuzzy filter around your engine? Or do you want to know what's going on in your organization? You can make it happen if you want to. Nothing is holding you back!

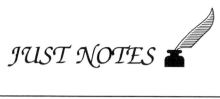

JUST NOTES

_____

_____

_____

_____

_____

_____

_____

"*As a general rule, the most successful man in life is the man who has the best information.*"

Benjamin Disraeli

_____

_____

_____

_____

_____

_____

_____

_____

_____

_____

_____

_____

_____

Competition
or Cooperation?

When does competition hurt more than it helps in the work-world? I often hear managers describe themselves as competitive. What does that mean? Does being competitive mean we run over our own players to get to the goal line, or does it mean we may lay down the perfect block to allow another player to score the touchdown? Competitiveness in and of itself is not necessarily a positive trait. Nor is it negative. Like many characteristics, it depends on how we use it.

Have you ever stopped to consider when you are competing with someone, that you're hoping they lose? And they're hoping you lose. On the other hand, when you're cooperating with someone, you're hoping they win and they're pulling for you. It's been my experience we could use a lot more cooperation and a little less competition in the workplace. In a competitive situation, everyone tends to jockey for position. In a cooperative situation, everyone on the team looks out for each other, thus everybody wins. Most of us were taught from childhood to be competitive: beat the other person, get the highest grades, drive the biggest car, and live in the best neighborhood.

Where do we learn the skills of cooperation? Team sports are probably the first organized experience most of us have in cooperation. Basketball, football, baseball, soccer, hockey—all these require cooperative teamwork. It's essential if the team is going to establish a winning tradition.

Some progressive school systems across the United States are now finding students learn better and faster in cooperative groups. The children work together to get the correct answers. But more importantly, they work as a team to understand the answer they've discovered. The process of interacting with others for a common goal requires logic and cooperation. It would seem to me we'd all reach our goals sooner if we cooperated more and competed less.

Let me introduce you to a concept practiced by many leaders. I have coined a word for this concept: "co-opetition." This word represents the best of both the cooperative and the competitive spirits. A synonym for co-opetition is *teamwork*. Co-opetition is practiced daily by people who really understand what teamwork, integrity, and winning are all about. In the '90s, it is even more important we address the spirit of co-opetition. We need to learn how to live it and establish it as the foundation of our teams in the workplace. Groups that practice interdependent co-opetition produce better goods and services. Also they have fun on their jobs, plus create and add real value in their places of work.

We can all practice healthy, honest competition while cooperating with others to help them achieve their goals. But leaders must first create an environment where the marriage of competition and cooperation can flourish. As a leader, what do you practice: competition or co-opetition?

JUST NOTES

_____

_____

_____

_____

_____

_____

_____

_____

"When love and skill work together, expect a masterpiece."

John Ruskin

_____

_____

_____

_____

_____

_____

_____

_____

_____

_____

_____

_____

_____

Are You a One Brainer?

I was a young manager fresh out of college in the early 1970s, full of vim and vigor. I mean I was ready to go get mine, and nothing or nobody was going to stop me. I was an interesting case study!

At one of our management meetings a corporate memo was read, "We will no longer *tell* our employees (as they were called then) what to do. Instead we will *ask* them to do what we want done.

This was simple—ask versus tell. Let employees feel as though they don't have to do it our way, so, even when they eventually do, they will feel better about it.

"This must be the new way to manage," I thought. *"Yeah—ask, not tell—I like that."*

So I started asking everybody to do it *my way* instead of telling them to do it *my way*. Brilliant. Of course, at that time in my life, I didn't have enough sense to realize we were only playing management games to keep the unions off balance. Nothing changed in management's mentality about leadership. "Con people into thinking they count and are being listened to" was management's way of retaining control.

Today I look back on those early days of behavior management and all the fads that came and went like the wind. It intrigues me just how gullible we actually were. We were *one braining* it. By that I mean I have one brain, and if I do something my way, with no input from the experts on the job, I'm one braining it. Not too smart.

Since then I have learned the value of *total braining*. When there is an opportunity or a problem, I solicit input from a team of experts—the people doing the job. I listen to them. We literally bond our brains together into a WHOLE, TOTAL brain and *the force is with us*. If I'm working with nine other people, and we total brain it, we do *it* much more effectively.

I've concluded that most managers are one-brainers by observing their behavior on the job. *Talking* total-brain leadership is very different from actually practicing it. Do you run a one-brain shop or a total-brain outfit? It's a simple but profound question each *leader* must ask if he or she is to be the best. In the 1990s, *real* leaders will choose to work with a total-brain mentality!

JUST NOTES

_____

_____

_____

_____

_____

_____

_____

_____

"I never learn anything talking. I only learn things when I ask questions."

Lou Holtz

_____

_____

_____

_____

_____

_____

_____

_____

_____

_____

_____

_____

_____

The Chance of a Lifetime

As a boy, I held several part-time jobs. At 14 I became the assistant janitor for our church. Every day when school let out I'd clean up after the kindergarten children, mop the floors, clean the restrooms, wipe the tables, and pick up so Mrs. Nichols, the kindergarten teacher, would have a clean place to conduct her classes the next morning. I especially liked my once-a-week job of waxing the floors and seeing them shine.

Saturday was my busiest day. I would arrive early to ready the church for Sunday services. I'd mop all floors, wax some on a rotation basis, wash windows, and mow the lawn—come rain or shine. I especially enjoyed cutting the beautiful green grass, much of which I had planted. After mowing the lawn, I'd get my hand shears and crawl around the foundation of our large church, clipping the grass I couldn't reach with my lawn mower. Then I would trim around each tree and shrub.

When finished, I'd often take my fishing pole and go to a local stream to see if the fish were biting.

Those beautiful days from 1959 to 1965 are forever etched in my mind. My salary of $1.25 an hour was good money then. I began learning to manage my income at an early age, saving 50 cents and spending 75. This was the beginning of a habit I still practice today, although I must admit the percentage saved has dropped.

As good as those years were, I later realized I had literally missed the chance of a lifetime. You see, *I didn't invent the Weed Eater*! I crawled around for miles with my hand-held clippers, and I had holes in my jeans to prove it. Yet I never stopped to ask, "Is there a better way to do this?" I had the need, I had the fishing line—all I lacked was the idea. But no one was there to challenge me and encourage me to think of a better way.

Today in companies across America, I often hear management comment on getting "crazy" ideas from employees who are involved in continuous improvement processes. It seems that many of them fail to realize that in order to get one fantastic *Weed Eater* idea (which will allow them to take a quantum leap past the competition) it may require a thousand non-Weed Eater ideas, even some crazy, undoable ones.

Roger Milliken, CEO of Milliken & Company and winner of the Malcolm Baldrige National Quality Award, says there are three problems facing American business that stand in the way of progress. They are: 1. Top management, 2. Middle management, and 3. Front-line management.

When will we learn to listen to the *experts* crawling around the foundations where we work—doing the nitty gritty clipping jobs—and challenge them to think of new and better ways to cut the grass?

The next time you look at your employees, just think of all the Weed-Eater ideas they have stored in their heads—ideas which can help trim costs and improve quality and customer service. They are the experts and it's a leader's responsibility to grow, nurture, and solicit their ideas, then follow through on them. It's up to you as a leader to develop the environment where this creative thinking can flourish.

Why not create your own *Weed Eater award* for the best idea implemented in your organization each year? Aren't you tired of crawling around wearing holes in the knees of your pants?

JUST NOTES

_____

_____

_____

_____

_____

_____

_____

_____

"The most valuable 100 people to bring into a deteriorating society would not be 100 chemists, or politicians, or professors, or engineers, but rather 100 entrepreneurs."

Abraham H. Marlow

_____

_____

_____

_____

_____

_____

_____

_____

_____

_____

_____

_____

"Good Help
Is Hard to Find"

This statement is more often than not a self-fulfilling prophecy. If an employer anticipates a prospective employee to be average or below, chances are that's exactly what the perception will be. We usually can only *see* what we expect.

During the '90s in the United States, a change as we've never seen before will occur in the demographics of the workplace. The authoritarians (born before 1929) will near extinction—the depression generation (1929-1945) will start to fade from the workplace. The baby-boomers will begin assuming the "watch" in America. But most important, the generation of the info-child (1965-present)—which none of the previous really understands—*is* the new talent of the '90s.

How do we respond to this reality? Do we sit around and bemoan how nobody's any good? Do we cry in our beer and talk about the "good old days?" Too often, people in responsible positions react this way to the changing labor market.

Perhaps a more insightful statement would be, "Good leaders are hard to find." Good leaders are those individuals who are willing to invest in people because they realize a company's greatest asset is the people it employs.

People want to succeed—not fail. Most people want to work for someone who has a genuine interest in their future—someone who truly cares about both their personal and professional development. In the U.S., nearly half of the incoming workforce between 18 and 25 years of age are products of broken homes. What an opportunity for *good* companies, large and small. They can develop in the workplace the family relationship often lacking at home.

When a person really feels needed, challenged, wanted, and loved in the workplace, he or she is much more likely to add value to the company. A nurtured associate tends to stay long-term with the employer. Zig Ziglar, author and motivational speaker, says it beautifully: "People don't care how much you know until they know how much you care." Think about that.

It may be difficult to find good help, but good leaders in management may be even harder to find. Are you a leader looking for people to nurture, respect, and challenge? Or do you simply employ *bodies* to fill slots in an attempt to accomplish the task? There is a BIG difference in the two. If you are a *true leader*, perhaps good help will not be so hard to find. Competent people may seek you out and want to work with you!

JUST NOTES

"Repeat anything long enough and it will become true."

Tom Hopkins

On Competence

Observation #1—in smaller, well-run companies, it's very difficult for marginal or poor performers to hide. Their attitude towards fellow associates and competence on the job are apparent to all.

It has been my experience that smaller companies are likely to deal with marginal and poor performers in a *proactive* manner. The solution can take many forms. Often more training or education is required to grow the marginal and poor performers into productive team members. If additional training does not help the situation, it may be necessary to change assignments or as a last resort, change players.

Observation #2—in larger companies, it's very difficult for marginal or poor performers to hide. Their attitude and competence are obvious. But here's where the story changes.

Larger companies are *NOT* as likely to deal with marginal or poor performers in a proactive manner. Often corporate lawyers and human resource policy manuals leave management hamstrung and unable to deal effectively with the problem.

Recommendation—large companies also need to deal head on with problem associates. Just as a good coach doesn't allow one or two players to ruin the team, a good leader will bench chronic problem associates, or send them home with a one-way ticket.

Question—are you ready to deal with problem associates? Or will you keep asking your good team members to carry an extra load? Don't procrastinate. Your company . . . and our country can't afford to wait!

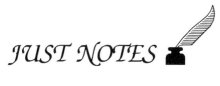

JUST NOTES

_____

_____

_____

_____

_____

_____

_____

_____

"It is not fair to ask of others what you are not willing to do yourself."

Eleanor Roosevelt

_____

_____

_____

_____

_____

_____

_____

_____

_____

_____

_____

_____

_____

_____

Waiting for the Wind

While vacationing on the coast of Maine, I had the pleasure of sailing on the 1918 schooner, *Surprise.* Captain Jack and Barbara Moore are a delightful couple who operate a day-sailing business in Penobscot Bay, Camden, Maine.

We were fortunate to have excellent weather that May day. The sun shone warmly on us while we slipped past islands with lighthouses and seals. A gentle wind and full sails were all we needed to take us to our points of interest.

Sailors like Barb and Jack take great pride in using no motors to assist them in their journeys. But while no motor may be fine for a skillful sailor, it doesn't bode well for ordinary folks. Ordinary people need motors. Our nation desperately needs people who will crank up their motors, define their purpose and mission, and then steer to their chosen ports of call.

No one can do it for us. We must each take it upon ourselves to chart our course and motor to our destination in life. Too many folks just sit and wait for the wind!

JUST NOTES

_____

_____

_____

_____

_____

_____

_____

_____

"If a man knows not what harbor he seeks, any wind is the right wind."

Seneca

_____

_____

_____

_____

_____

_____

_____

_____

_____

_____

_____

_____

_____

The Queen Is Leaving

My cousin was graduating from the Medical University of South Carolina in Charleston with a pharmacy degree. Her parents, two other family members, and I drove down from the mountains of South Carolina to our *mother* city to celebrate the occasion.

While checking into our hotel on Thursday afternoon we learned the luxury liner, *Queen Elizabeth II*, was in port only three blocks away. We met the soon-to-be graduate and her husband, and together enjoyed a wonderful meal within sight of the huge ship.

Our meal finished, we returned to our hotel room at 10:30 P.M. and swapped more stories and shared more laughter. Then we got the idea of walking the three blocks to the ocean liner to behold its midnight departure on a Caribbean cruise.

At 11:00 P.M. the docks were crowded with onlookers as the beautiful ship blazed with light. Passengers lined the decks. We watched as scores of others rejoined the ship after a night on the town. Midnight approached. The crowd became excited in anticipation of the *Queen's* departure. Noisy activity ensued as the huge hawsers were released and drawn into the ship's hull. Tugboats disappeared from view as they assumed their places on the harbor side of the ship, ready to gently ease her from the dock.

Finally at 12:10 A.M., the *Queen* gave three loud blasts from her horns. Chills ran down my spine as the mammoth ship backed ever so slowly from the dock. Three more blasts from the horn and we could clearly see the giant slip into the harbor. Then the *Queen Elizabeth II* slowly maneuvered out of sight behind other docked ships.

To my amazement, the crowd began to disperse. This magnificent ship had yet to leave the harbor. How could these people be leaving now? Sleep comes every night, but the *QE II* may come only once in a lifetime.

My party realized the show was just beginning. All five of us, ages 25 to 75, hurried off the dock and up the 100 or so stairs to the entrance of the beautiful old marble U.S. Customs House. From there we had a marvelous view of the *Queen*, led by the harbor pilot's tugboat, making her way into the open harbor and slipping quietly into the darkness of the Atlantic Ocean. We stood in silence as this huge ship became only a star on the horizon.

What an experience! It was past 1:00 A.M. when we began the short stroll to our hotel. As we walked, I realized 98% of the people, some of whom had waited for hours to see this historic but brief visitor to Charleston, had missed the *real show*. They had shown up and left—*quit*—just before the most beautiful and mystical moment.

I find this to be true in life as well. So many times we strive for something—only to quit when one more month, week, day, hour, minute, or . . . tick of the clock would have given us our dream. There's a lot to be said for patience . . . and persistence. There is pitifully little of it taught—and less practiced—in our culture today.

Keep on course. Stay with your task until it is finished and *your* bright light joins the stars on the horizon!

JUST NOTES

"*Success seems to be largely a matter of hanging on after others have let go.*"

William Feather

Climbing Life Mountain

I was born on a cold December day in 1946 in the South Carolina foothills of the Blue Ridge Mountains. Since that day I've been climbing my mountain. The name of that mountain is Life. Life Mountain is so high we can never see the top. In fact, it seems to go on forever even though we know it can't.

We spend 99.9% of our lives on the side, not the top, of this mountain. The .1% represents "the top." When we reach it, one of two things happens: we either die or stop growing personally and professionally. Perhaps we should stop and think about these alternatives. Then as we approach each day's climb, we would obviously work on improving ourselves personally and professionally. The higher we climb, the more spectacular the view.

Since we spend the majority of our time on the side of Life Mountain, shouldn't we enjoy the climb? Too many people never take their eyes off what they perceive to be the top of the mountain. They never stop to look around, smell the roses, and enjoy the marvelous view available every day.

Most people seem to survive only by making a mad dash toward the top of Life Mountain each day. They hope they will finally be happy and find joy in their lives when they arrive. Little children, teenagers, mothers, fathers, businessmen and women—everyone seems to be heading at breakneck speed towards the top. They never stop to appreciate the surrounding scenery, and certainly not to just enjoy the *journey*.

"The top" means different things to different people—when we get the kids through college, when we get the house paid for, when we retire, when we get the money—definitions are endless.

Actually, on Life Mountain there need not be a top! I hope I have the courage in my life to continue to climb, to enjoy the view along the way, and to become more than I am now.

Are you enjoying your climb up Life Mountain? Did you appreciate yesterday's climb? How about today's? Did you stop to look at the view? Working only to reach *the top* is not living—it is merely surviving.

Let me challenge you to turn around on the side of your Mountain and just sit for awhile and enjoy the scenery. This is life; this may be as good as it gets. You and I may have many more days to climb. Then again, this may be our last.

Learning to treat each day as if we're already on the top is a wonderful way to live on Life Mountain, for in reality, each day is *the top*, or could be.

Want to borrow my binoculars? The view today is fantastic. Take a good look and really enjoy. You're seeing life, my friend, that most wonderful gift of all!

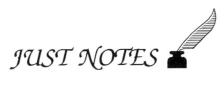

JUST NOTES

_____

_____

_____

_____

_____

_____

_____

_____

"To live for some future goal is shallow. It's the sides of the mountain that sustain life, not the top."

Robert M. Pirsig

_____

_____

_____

_____

_____

_____

_____

_____

_____

_____

_____

_____

_____

The Gift of Time

Dad was excited long before I arrived to take him on a trip to Colorado as a Father's Day treat. A 44-year-old Santa Claus gave his dad one of those wonderful open-ended presents that read: "A trip to anywhere with your son, all expenses paid." Dad chose Colorado for our adventure together. Seventy-three years young, he was still full of enthusiasm and curiosity about a gift he'd received more than seven decades ago—the gift of life.

We packed, drove to Atlanta, and flew first class to Denver. Dad had never flown before. His excitement was touching and contagious. The two stewardesses on our flight immediately fell in love with this *real person* I was traveling with. He kept his eyes glued to the window for most of the two-and-a-half-hour flight. He loved it."Smooth as silk," he kept repeating. He even relaxed enough to enjoy a short nap during the flight.

Landing in Denver, we rented a car and headed for Vail, where my wife, Kathy, and I had skied a few months earlier. On the drive over I-70 to Vail, Dad exclaimed at every view of snow-in-June, "Son look, there's some on the side of the road!"

During the next three days, we talked of things we'd never talked about before. We shared things that neither of us knew about our childhood and our manhood.

A mile chair-lift ride to the top of Beaver Creek Resort was an experience Dad was especially proud of. He was thrilled that the "pretty young girl," as he called the chair-lift attendant, let him ride free because he was over 70 years old. As we approached the top on that beautiful, cool, windy day, he told me, "I guess not many folks over 70 do this kind of thing but I highly recommend they try it—to keep them young, Joe." I took several pictures of him on the lift trip because he wanted his family to see he wasn't exaggerating his adventure.

That evening we enjoyed a good meal and a cozy fire at our condo. Dad, a weather nut, kept checking the thermometer on the patio and gleefully reporting the temperature back to me. Then it was off to a dreamy sleep with the peaceful sound of a river outside our window.

I awoke next morning to the aroma of coffee. Dad was up having his brand of cereal with the milk he'd bought and the sugar he'd borrowed from the restaurant the night before.

"Ready to go, boy? I've been up since 5:00 A.M.!"

"Yes, sir," I replied. "How did you sleep?"

"Like a baby."

We drove over the pass toward Leadville and on to Buena Vista to meet some dear friends Kathy and I had made while writing my first book, *The Attitude Connection*. Dad was amazed by the scenery. We stopped so he could make a snowball. He ran down a small hill to a drift three feet deep at such a rapid pace I thought he was going to dive into it. He posed proudly with his June snowball as I snapped his picture. Following him toward another drift, a tear appeared in my eye in sheer appreciation for this man I owe so much to and love so dearly.

We returned to the car and drove on to a beautiful valley where Kathy and I had purchased some acreage for our future mountain home. Dad walked the 6.5 acres, marveling at the 360 degree views of the valley and snowcapped Rockies.

"Here is where I'd put my cabin, Joe. I hope to God I live to see you kids build it. I'll come and stay with you and help out some. There's a lot of work you'll want to do on the land." Then he walked through the wild flowers and aspens to the creek that borders our land. "I'm happy for you, son, really happy," he said hugging me.

We drove into Buena Vista and met my dear friends, Tom and Marilyn Ross. We had lunch with them, toured their home under construction, and then headed for Colorado Springs. We followed the Arkansas River through the magnificent rocky canyons. In a couple of hours or so we reached Colorado Springs where we got rooms at the Hilton. Dad searched the local phone book and located the son of an old friend who'd graduated from the Air Force Academy in 1959. He called him and they had a thirty-minute reunion over the phone. We got to bed early after relishing another great Colorado day.

The next morning after breakfast, we visited the Garden of the Gods. Dad had to have his picture taken next to Balanced Rock. It astonished him, as it does everyone, that the boulder doesn't tip over.

Our next stop was the Professional Rodeo Hall of Fame. We enjoyed the visit and Dad met a woman whose daughter was riding in the rodeo finals. He soon discovered this lady was the daughter of an old friend from Clemson, South Carolina!

The U.S. Air Force Academy in Colorado Springs absolutely blew my father's mind. We stopped again and again and again for pictures. The football stadium prompted many a story from Dad about all the games he'd watched on TV which had been "played in a blizzard." After a stop at the visitors' center and an inspiring walk through the famous chapel, we were off to Denver.

We had another delightful dinner, which by now had become sharing sessions about the past, present, and future. There were stories about mother and dad riding ferris wheels while dating—how his hair was blond as a boy before it turned black, tales of his trip in 1927 to New York City with his father, and more.

Father's Day 1991, we awoke to a clear, cool morning in Denver. We relaxed awhile after breakfast, then headed for Stapleton Airport just across the street from our hotel. After another beautiful flight to Atlanta, we drove back home to South Carolina.

There are no words to describe this experience with my father. There was no emotion left untouched within me. No one can *make* us take some time for our parents. The pictures, memories, and time spent together will be cherished forever by this son and his dad.

Don't wait! We only visit with each other on this planet for a split second in time. What a shame if you miss this tiny window of opportunity! Make the time to "do" something with someone you love. It will be a present impossible to wrap—for there's not enough paper and ribbon in the world to cover love!

JUST NOTES

_____

_____

_____

_____

_____

_____

_____

_____

"Regret for time wasted can become a power for good in the time that remains. And the time that remains is enough."

Arthur Brisbane

_____

_____

_____

_____

_____

_____

_____

_____

_____

_____

_____

_____

The Busy Disease

Most people believe they don't have enough time in today's busy world. I hear everywhere, "I don't have time to do this or that." There are thousands of reasons why people honestly believe they can't do something or accomplish a given task. We often fall into the trap of using this trite statement as a convenient crutch for not accomplishing the required.

Everyone has the same 24 hours in each day. Why is it some people get so much accomplished and others so little? In searching for an answer, I decided to observe how successful people spend their time. I watched how they did things, I studied their habits, and I learned what skills they practiced to accomplish so much in relatively short periods of time. After a year or so of watching, listening, and asking questions of successful managers, I discovered there is one key to having enough time. The key is setting *priorities*.

Think about this:

Your grandmother or grandfather probably seemed to have more time to relax than you do. If your grandparents were like mine, I imagine that while they had a more demanding life in many ways, they also had a simpler life. For example, there were three major priorities in my grandparents' lives: family, church, and making a living—just three!

How many priorities do you try to balance? Family, friends, business, travel, all the kids' activities, church, civic groups, environmental causes, politics, entertainment, physical exercise, TV, yard work, household chores, hobbies, etc. Instead of three, you may have 20 or more.

The simple fact is—it is humanly impossible in today's world to do everything that seems to demand attention. It simply can't be done. Successful time managers realize this and prioritize. They decide what is most important to them and then focus on these few vital things. If we try to do it all, we will do nothing well.

You'll notice I did not list rest or think-time as a priority ball we keep in the air. We often forget we need rest and meditation as well as physical activity. Recently I read that a poll taken in the United States revealed that many people feel guilty when they rest. For some reason, we've grown to think that our body machine never needs a tune up. We simply drive it until the engine blows up!

Setting priorities is essential if we are to excel at any given task or if we are to accomplish our goals in life. Without a priority mentality, people tend to burn out. We must learn to be aware of this modern-day phenomenon, which I call the "busy disease."

Most people find time to do what is important to them. For example, we usually find time to play golf or tennis, but do not find time to visit our parents or mow the lawn. That's because one is more important to us than the other. We may not like to admit it, but it's true.

Since there seems to be general agreement that we truly can't "do it all," perhaps we need to focus on exactly what is most important in our lives. I suggest we write our priorities clearly on a piece of paper, discuss them with our associates and our families, then *make* time to do them. Successful time managers practice this exercise.

Trusting others, which leads to delegating responsibilities, can also be a key factor in learning to enjoy life and in becoming more successful. You and I *do* have enough time! The problem is that we want to "do it all, all the time." When you are asked to do something, learn to say, "I'd really like to; however, I have other priorities now that require my time." That's a nice way to say NO. As long as we try to say YES to everything, we're digging a deeper and deeper time-hole.

No one is immune to the busy disease. Sitting in my house one Sunday afternoon, I felt frustrated when I realized I couldn't ride my horse, go swimming in our friends' pool, work out, and read the *New York Times* in one afternoon. If I did, it would make work out of what should be leisure time. Do you find yourself in similar situations in your professional and personal life? I'll bet you do.

My advice is to do fewer things really well, enjoy them, and throw away your guilt baggage. Let's agree—many good things make demands on our time. We must decide what is and what is not important to us. Then we can get on with putting focus and joy back into our daily lives.

I never say to anyone, "I don't have enough time." Why? Because I do. It's up to me to make choices and to set my priorities. So let's throw down the time crutch and focus on setting effective priorities. We'll enjoy our lives more. And . . . we might even find a little extra time for ourselves!

JUST NOTES

_____

_____

_____

_____

_____

_____

_____

_____

_____

"It is not the man who has too little, but the man who craves more, that is poor."

Seneca

_____

_____

_____

_____

_____

_____

_____

_____

_____

_____

_____

_____

_____

_____

_____

A Bermuda Christmas

Christmas in Bermuda was such a memorable holiday for Kathy, her mother, and me. We intended to escape the hustle and bustle of the U.S. Christmas season as well as leave our familiar home surroundings. Kathy's father had died a few months earlier, so we reasoned it would be easier to get through our first Christmas without him by taking a trip.

Kathy and I had visited Bermuda some eight Decembers before and found it to be a lovely place with beautiful pink beaches and polite people. All Bermudians seem to understand tourism is their life blood. And they treat their visitors accordingly. More importantly, they genuinely seem to enjoy it.

Arriving at the airport, we took a taxi to the Hamilton Princess Hotel where we had rooms for the week of Christmas. The hotel had a splendid array of activities for all ages during the holiday week. Most of the hotel guests and other tourists were mature adults. The summer yuppies were absent, much to my delight.

I found my American rush-rush mentality began to slowly fade into a more relaxed frame of mind. By Christmas Eve, we were beginning to understand that the Bermudians truly do make the time to enjoy the holiest of seasons. The shops along Front Street began closing early on Christmas Eve as owners and workers alike hurried home to be with their families.

The local radio and television stations played wonderful Christmas songs, many of which I hadn't heard since childhood.

Splendid old songs from the 1940s and 1950s peppered the radio waves as well.

The Bermuda television station featured video recordings of several local schools' Christmas programs. The Hamilton Christmas parade was shown, as well as several church services that had taken place prior to Christmas Day. Messages were given to the people of Bermuda from Queen Elizabeth, the Governor of Bermuda, and the Premier of Bermuda. Their words were filled with thanksgiving and hope for the future. It was a very pleasant change from the consistently negative slant of the U.S. news media.

All this focus on the positive made me wonder what would happen if the American media gave the positive things in life equal time with the negative? Perhaps there would be a rebirth of hope in the youth of our country. I have observed we may be raising a generation of negative thinkers. When there is so little hope among the young, there isn't much of a future for them.

I awoke to a divine sunrise Christmas morning. After breakfast, Santa Claus arrived at the front of the hotel by horse-drawn carriage. Children of hotel guests were invited to ride around the circular driveway with Santa, as were our special guests from a local primary school chorus.

As Santa entered the hotel lobby, we followed the jolly old elf to the second floor grand ballroom. The room was invitingly decked out with a huge Christmas tree, under which were presents for all the children. The Queen herself looked approvingly on the scene from her portrait over the fireplace. Santa presented gifts to each child as he or she sat on his knee. The entire affair reminded me of Bing Crosby's wonderful movie, *Holiday Inn*, in which he first sang my favorite Christmas carol, "White Christmas."

The children's chorus from the Dellwood Primary School entertained us with religious carols as their teacher narrated the Christmas story. Following this sweet, touching presentation, we all joined together and sang more carols. Here we were—citizens of the world—singing together and having a wonderful time. The Christmas spirit was truly in everyone's hearts.

On December 26, I enjoyed an early morning walk in downtown Hamilton, the capital of Bermuda. All businesses and stores were still closed, as it was Boxing Day. In the Commonwealth, Boxing Day is a traditional holiday originally observed to give household staff gifts and a day off from work. Bermudians take this holiday seriously. Only a few motor scooters and taxis were in the streets. The harbor was deserted except for two tugboats, the Faithful and the Forceful. A smaller boat was also on duty awaiting a cargo ship which was to arrive that morning. Otherwise, there was no activity on the docks. I reflected on what it must be like back in the United States on this day after Christmas. The "greed seed" hasn't grown as well on the islands as it has on the mainland.

The ferries were running on their holiday schedule. I stopped at the terminal long enough to visit four natives readying to board—they were going to visit their grandmother in St. George, just at the tip of the island.

Kathy, her mother, and I enjoyed several more days and watched the normal pace of daily life resume. I found that a true sense of community exists in Bermuda which has been lost in much of our country. There is a sense of family, of tradition, and a love of life lacking in much of the U.S.

Traveling throughout our great country, which I love dearly, affords me the opportunity to meet many people. Most business people I meet tell me they are not really very happy. Why should this be so? Perhaps unlike my Bermuda "friends," we're simply too busy. There's also a deep rent in the fabric of the American family; over half our children are products of broken homes. The emotional carnage left by this scar will affect our nation for generations.

At my age, I've come to a conclusion about life: You can have *anything* you want but you cannot have *everything* you want! Got that?

Setting priorities is something each person must do. My generation and those following need to step back from the rat race and decide what is really important. Three cars in every garage allow each working parent to drive to work and the children can take the third to their therapist! Both parents working outside the home allows children to have the best things money can buy.

In the good ole USA we can have it all. But, mother *and* father must both work full time, beating their brains out so there will be enough money for them and their children to have it *all*.

My late father-in-law understood what really counted in life. He was living proof you can be a successful business person and still be a wonderful father, husband, father-in-law, and friend. Life is sweet but so very short. Perhaps we should stop long enough to take stock of what our priorities are before it's too late.

If we had but one car per household—as they do in Bermuda— perhaps we might just learn to ride together in harmony!

JUST NOTES

"What does it profit a man [or country] if he gains the whole world but loses his own soul?"

The Holy Bible

A Simple Halloween

I had raked leaves in my yard twice that October week. Now the yard wanted me to scratch its back again. So I dragged the rake over it, collecting the dry, feather-light leaves.

It was that wonderful time of year we all look forward to. The holidays were approaching: Halloween, Thanksgiving, Christmas, New Year's, and hopefully a winter snow. This year, the lady of our house purchased a big orange pumpkin at the local market. I came home from work and saw it on the kitchen table. It was a handsome specimen sitting by the knives that would soon transform it into a jack-o-lantern.

Two days passed and the pumpkin remained on the table. No one had done the deed. Several more days passed and I found myself thinking about performing the surgery on the pumpkin myself. I was not worried about my ineptness as a surgeon, for my technique would inflict no pain on this inanimate object.

Someone needed to take up the scalpel and mold the pumpkin into what it was intended to be—a Halloween jack-o-lantern signaling to all who passed that treats were waiting behind our red front door. This year, instead of a plastic or ceramic thing lit by a flashlight, we'd have a real jack-o-lantern on our steps. It would be the scariest in the neighborhood! I asked Kathy for her assistance. She placed newspapers on the counter under the pumpkin and helped me hold it as I outlined with a Magic Marker what I hoped to be a masterpiece. Finished with the drawing, I secured a sharp knife and made my first incision, cutting off the top and then picking it up by the large stem. Beautiful!

Setting the top aside, I put my hands into the pumpkin, feeling the seeds and hundreds of stringy, slimy tentacles connected to the interior. I pulled out handful after handful until it was almost clean.

Carefully rolling up the paper, I put the contents into the waste basket and washed my hands much as a surgeon would. Approaching the patient, I was now ready for the carving. My work of art began to take shape, first with perfect triangular eyes, then a triangular nose, followed by a snaggle-tooth smile. I could hardly wait to put it outside.

We found a large fat candle and secured it in the bottom of our handsome jack-o-lantern. We were delighted with the outcome! Our three cocker spaniels, who had supervised the entire affair, were sniffing and wagging their tails excitedly.

When darkness fell, we placed our treasure on the front steps. After lighting the candle and putting the top back on, we stood back—dogs and all—to admire the effect. Perfect! The holiday season was officially launched.

I asked Kathy if she would drive me by our house in our family pick-up truck. We loaded our three cockers and off we went, being careful not to even glance toward the house as we left. We wanted to drive away, turn around, and ride by as if we were just passing.

Here we came, three cocker spaniels and two excited humans just rounding the bend to our home. There it was. It looked great. The dogs jumped with glee and we laughed at how much fun it was and how we would do it every year.

Life seemed so simple. We took time to rejoice in the little things. Why don't most folks take the time to look, to be, to do, and to enjoy? To be over 40 and have this childlike experience was wonderful.

Psychiatrists tell us we need to release that wee person within to do and savor the things we did as children. Why not? When was the last time you did a childlike thing? Liberate that wonderful little person and integrate him or her back into who you are. There are so many wonderful experiences awaiting when you do!

JUST NOTES

"Childhood sometimes does pay a second visit to a man; youth never."

Jameson

Just Thoughts

The more people you meet, the more people you'll meet.

Do unto others as they would want done unto them, not as you want done unto you! There's usually a *big* difference.

After returning from a four weeks' vacation in 1991, the President of the United States said he'd come to the conclusion that "American kids watch entirely too much television." Wow, he noticed! Studies have shown for years that most high school graduates spent several thousands more hours watching the boob tube than in the classroom listening to their teachers.

We've heard all our lives we are what we eat. Perhaps we are also what we see, hear—and believe. The nation's violent crime statistics seem to bear this out. But isn't TV a great babysitter?

If a poisonous snake is on the steps leading to your garage, you don't just knock it off and let it crawl under the car only to reappear and bite you. The same is true with problems at work. Finish them off—don't let them keep crawling back.

The older I get, the more I understand one of the greatest gifts you can give another person is honesty—especially when it hurts.

Someone once told me that money can't buy happiness. "That's right," I agreed then added, "but neither can poverty!"

Most folks feel it is important to treat everyone fairly—and the same. I disagree. Effective leaders know you must treat everyone fairly—and *differently*.

A. Grade School |
    High School | =   Formal Education
    College |

B. Life School You never graduate.
              You just keep learning.

    Formula: $A + B^2$ = Likely to succeed
                 $A^2 + B$ = Not likely to succeed

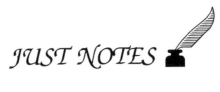

JUST NOTES

"The difference between failure and success is doing a thing nearly right and doing it exactly right."

Edward C. Simmons

No, I Don't Have a Card

Ever been to Des Moines, Iowa? Well, I have. The American Feed Industry Association was kind enough to have me as the keynote speaker for their Regional Production School. The second I stepped from the plane, I sensed it was a good place to be: clean air, friendly people at the airport, polite people everywhere I went.

One delightful gentleman I met was Ray Hines, the 71-year-old airport shoeshine man. He told me how he'd moved to Michigan from Texas as a boy. He went on to tell me how he'd been shining shoes in Des Moines for over twenty years. Ray is a smart man. He keeps up with just about everything, especially politics. I asked Ray if he had a business card and he said, "No." I got his address so I could write him a note of thanks.

On the way to the University Holiday Inn I was driven by Howard, a native Iowan in his sixties. He, too, was very friendly and helpful. When I asked if he had a business card he replied, "No."

After being checked in by three very nice young desk clerks, I stopped by the concierge's desk and met Amy (again no card). I asked her to schedule a riding tour of Des Moines for eight the next morning. Ten minutes later, Amy called my room to tell me about the tour arrangements.

"Mr. Black, Jeff Murra will meet you at 8:00 A.M. tomorrow and drive you around Des Moines in the airport shuttle. Will that be okay?" I replied that I was looking forward to it.

The next morning, Jeff arrived at 8:00 A.M. sharp. As we pulled away in the green Holiday Inn van, he asked, "Mr. Black, what do you want to see? I've never had anyone ask for a tour before."

I replied, "Anything of interest. Just drive around and show me what you'd show your best friend if he or she were visiting for the first time. I appreciate your time, and I'm already enjoying your company as well as the scenery."

Jeff Murra gave me a one hour, fifteen minute tour that was fantastic! He showed me the Triple A Cubs ballpark, the capitol, old Des Moines, and everything in between. I learned Jeff, his wife, and his son, Kirby, had just moved back two years earlier after being in Reno, Nevada, for eight years. He explained the people in Iowa were family oriented and trusted each other. He and his wife wanted their son to be brought up in a place "where people really care about each other."

After the tour, I thanked Jeff and handed him a tip, which he refused. He simply would not hear of it. So I told him, "Alright, I'm not giving the money to you. I'm giving it to Kirby. Buy him a present with it. Now that's that!" Reluctantly, he accepted the tip. I asked Jeff if he had a business card, and he said, "No." So I got his address—same story.

That afternoon, I met over two hundred wonderful people—grain and feed producers from all over the midwest. No cards? Right! Have you ever stopped to realize some of the nicest people you meet don't have business cards? They're just there, doing their jobs, raising their families, living their lives—adding value to our nation.

Next time you're on the road, take the time to talk with, listen to, and love all those folks with no cards. They're the best!

JUST NOTES

"I weigh the man, not his title; 'tis not the king's stamp can make the metal better."

Wycherly

Do We Still Want
a Thanksgiving Day?

It seems to me we missed the boat during the Thanksgiving season of 1991. I had the opportunity to travel quite a bit during that particular holiday. My travels took me to many points in the USA.

Talk of how bad things were in our economy headlined every national news broadcast. Dirty politics in Washington, D.C. was featured in almost every newspaper I read. People everywhere seemed down on all elected officials. Print and electronic media churned out anything negative they could dig up about anybody and anything in Washington. Never mind if it was true or not; if it was bad, then it appeared.

Just a year prior, our nation's and the world's total focus was on the accumulating cloud of Desert Storm in the middle east. All conversations across our America concentrated on the *big war* coming with Iraq. How could we forget so fast? Why was our country and our culture not remembering and celebrating the hundreds of thousands of Americans and Allied troops who had returned safely home after a military victory? No mention was made about the stock market being about 300 points higher than 12 months ago. The good news of America's families reducing their debt by spending less—and corporations reducing their inventories and debts—didn't make the newspaper, radio, or TV.

How come no news about the thousands of well-led companies that were doing well—even creating new jobs? There was no mention of the West winning the Cold War. Only negatives bombarded us from the media. Why, when there was so much to be thankful for?

I don't know the answer, but I have some questions. Could it be we actually enjoy bad news? Is it true that our culture thrives on bad news for some unknown reason?

Sure we face problems: health care, AIDS, unemployment, homeless people, crime, and corruption at all levels of government and business. We must focus on these issues and deal with them as a nation. But if people are not fed good news along with the bad, will they be willing or able to help themselves, much less others? I think not!

Hope—in our hearts and our minds—is necessary if we are to become the nation we could and should be. The news media and every American citizen need to understand that if we murder hope, there will be no chance to solve our problems and move forward.

So do we stick our heads in the sand and pretend all is well? Absolutely not! We must allow the wonderful things that occur in this world to get equal time in our media and most importantly in our *minds*.

Remember, if you eat unhealthy food all the time, you stay sick and will eventually die. We must take time to give thanks for our blessings and to plant and nurture hope. If our society doesn't take time to celebrate goodness and hope, it may lose the capability to celebrate at all!

JUST NOTES

_____

_____

_____

_____

_____

_____

_____

_____

"Pride slays Thanksgiving, but an humble mind is the soil out of which thanks naturally flow."

H.W. Beecher

_____

_____

_____

_____

_____

_____

_____

_____

_____

_____

_____

_____

_____

_____

Bowled Over

Mother is baking my birthday cake and preparing the chocolate icing. "Joe, do you want to sop (lick) the bowl? There's some icing left."

"Yes, yes!" I shout and dive for the bowl.

My mother provided this pre-birthday treat each year while I waited for the cake to be served with the appropriate number of candles. This annual delight (which I later referred to reverently as "the sopping of the bowl"), was thoroughly enjoyed by every taste bud in my body. My birthday falls just ten days prior to Christmas, just before our minds begin turning to another kind of bowl—the football bowls.

As I was a boy, I "sopped and licked" each one—the Rose Bowl (first played in 1902), the Cotton Bowl (originated in 1937), the Orange Bowl (begun in 1935), and the Sugar Bowl (first game in 1935). I knew who the players were, their teams' records, and I recalled the score of each game for months afterward. To play in a bowl in the 1950s really meant something. It was special.

Now there are 19 bowl games, almost as many as letters in the alphabet. If I tried to sop and lick every bowl game now, I no doubt would O.D. (overdose). You see, there are so many bowl games now they no longer have the same prestige they once had. Like birthday candles on a cake, too many can cause you to stop

---

counting. The light from the candles seems to blur into one big fire. You can't tell one candle from the other.

Too many bowls to sop and lick. The cake somehow doesn't seem to taste as good as it did before. Excess dulls any experience!

JUST NOTES

_____

_____

_____

_____

_____

_____

_____

_____

"Anything in excess leads to boredom and disinterest."

Anonymous

_____

_____

_____

_____

_____

_____

_____

_____

_____

_____

_____

_____

_____

Just One More Banana

A few years ago, the American public was urged by the first lady of our land to "Just Say No" to drugs. In real life, it is often very difficult to say "no"—or even "maybe." What looks good at first glance can turn out to be deadly.

In the business world, most of us have been trained to say "can do," not "no" or "maybe." One of the most difficult things for any business person wishing to help existing or potential customers achieve their goals is to say "no." Let me illustrate with a story.

Once upon a time there was a banana boat. It had an excellent reputation as one of the best ships afloat. Its crew was swelling with pride after many extremely successful voyages. Other ships and their crews were envious of this wonderful banana boat.

One day, she set sail with a full load. She plowed the seas day after day until another ship radioed for help. The wonderful ship quickly sailed to her troubled counterpart. The troubled ship wanted to improve *its* own efficiency by unloading some of its cargo onto the banana boat.

"Can you take some of our cargo?" asked the captain. "We'll pay you top dollar." The banana boat's skipper and crew really wanted to assist the distressed ship, but they were already full—taking an additional load could jeopardize their current customers.

They discussed their fellow ship's dilemma. "We're sorry but we're loaded down and can't take on any more cargo. We wish we could help, but we owe it to the clients who entrusted us with this premium load to deliver it safely and on time. We'll radio another ship to help you!"

The captain of the troubled ship was disappointed but understood that such dedication was the reason this was such a wonderful ship.

"Thank you for your interest in our service," said the skipper. "We appreciate your calling us. If you're still interested in a partnership after we fulfill our current obligations, we'll be happy to serve you."

Companies large and small could learn a valuable lesson here. Taking on more business than you can effectively service could *sink* you. Knowing when to say no is a vital key to leading a successful operation. Beware—*just one more banana* can sink a wonderful ship!

JUST NOTES

"Better shun the bait than struggle in the snare."

Dryden

Is Your Rudder In the Water?

Why do so many people with tremendous potential for success blow it—careers floundered, personal lives destroyed, good attitudes torpedoed, goals never set—much less achieved? Perhaps it's because they haven't kept their rudders in the water!

Your motor can be purring on all cylinders, but all you do is go around in circles without a rudder to give you direction. Life's rudder can take many forms. Some examples might be:

1) Loving family and friends

2) A spiritual foundation

3) A strong work ethic

4) Setting high goals for yourself

5) Not letting defeat break you

6) Visualizing where you want to be

7) Believing in yourself

8) Having a positive attitude

9) Helping others reach their dreams

10) Allowing yourself to be creative

11) Not asking or looking for approval when you know you're right

12) A clear set of values

13) Defining your purpose in life

Here are the keys:

First—define and build your rudders.

Second—be sure to keep them in the water and steer toward your vision.

You can control only yourself, no one else. Have you defined your rudder and are you keeping on course to reach a specific point on your horizon? Try it. You'll be surprised at what happens!

JUST NOTES

_____

_____

_____

_____

_____

_____

_____

_____

_____

"*A man without a purpose is like a ship without a rudder.*"

Thomas Carlyle

_____

_____

_____

_____

_____

_____

_____

_____

_____

_____

_____

_____

_____

Looking Back
On the Future

When I was in my late thirties, my visual depth perception on the tennis courts went south and stayed. After the yellow sphere began hitting my face as often as my racket, I decided to take up golf and leave tennis to my business partner, Pudge Tate.

Golf is a sport in which the ball is stationary, and it only takes a smooth clean swing to shoot like a pro. At least that's what all the videos, books, and golf instructors say.

As a fair weather golfer, I've explored several experts' advice on the game over the years. I purchased a Jack Nicklaus video which explained the secret of the game is to visualize the shot before you actually hit the ball. I practiced this technique and it really helped my game. (One friend I play with says he'd hate to see my score if I didn't visualize—as I still shoot 92 to 105 on any given day.)

Not long after I began practicing Mr. Nicklaus' advice on visualizing, I had the opportunity to attend a local golf clinic conducted by Gary Player. He too spoke of how you must *see it* happen before it actually takes place. Mr. Player blasted out of sand traps with amazing accuracy and consistency. Every shot found the ball in or close to the cup. It was unbelievable to see this champion working at his craft.

I excitedly drove to the golf course the very next day and shot an honest 92. I'd never broken 100! Then I asked myself a simple question: If this technique works so well in sports, why not in life? Guess what? . . . It does.

I began to realize I had been practicing visualization for years in my professional life. But it was subconscious—I had never stopped to think about it. Now I understand the importance of visualization and am studiously perfecting this skill.

When you have a very important meeting or presentation coming up, picture yourself as being the salvation for your clients and customers. Literally train your brain to visualize the event as though it *has already happened.* I call this phenomenon "looking back on the future" and I practice it every day.

As I drive to work, I look down on my car rolling along the highway as if I'm hovering high above it. I think, *"There you were, Joe. That was ten years ago, old boy. You were on your way to make a presentation to Acme Metals that day and you handled the situation like a pro. That was a good day in your life. You made a difference. You really helped those people."*

This habit of literally *looking back on the future* helps me keep things in perspective. Let's say I'm facing a difficult problem in my professional or personal life. I pull my mind up over me and my situation. Looking down from above, I see everything around me as it is and think, *"That was a tough one, Joe. It's hard to believe that was twenty years ago. You handled yourself admirably under the circumstances and I'm proud of you. If you were to do it over again though, you should take it less seriously and enjoy the day more."*

Now, before you label me as a candidate for the local loony bin or call for the men in the white coats, let me challenge you to try it. Don't knock it before you do. Visualize—look back on the future—and see events as though you've already lived through them *successfully.* It will help you set priorities in your life. It will also help you keep things in proper perspective.

Additionally it will serve as a very helpful tool to assess the next step in your career. Look back on the future of your present job. If you don't feel excited, take control of your life. Change it to be what you want it to be before your future becomes your past!

JUST NOTES

_____

_____

_____

_____

_____

_____

_____

_____

"The best way to predict the future is to invent it."

Anonymous

_____

_____

_____

_____

_____

_____

_____

_____

_____

_____

_____

_____

_____

Become Who You Are

Each of us is unique. Truly unique. God has given us different faces, talents, minds, and hearts. Unfortunately many people are uncomfortable with their individuality and adopt uniformity with everyone else. They hasten to follow the latest fashions and fads. When I was a teenager in the late '50s and early '60s, it was beatniks and hippies. Today's business men and women make a like statement with their *power* suits and ties and their yuppie mentality. Too many of us get caught in the *sameness* trap.

But I've noticed often the most interesting and successful people I've known have avoided being just like everybody else. They are individuals and proud of it. How did they do it? Perhaps they allowed themselves to become *who* they are. Got that? We must each become who we are if we're to reach our true potential.

To become who we are may require us to be somewhat of a free spirit. It means we do not *seek* others' approval for our actions or our thoughts. If our hearts and heads know it's right, then we should do it! This demands courage and a strong belief in *ourselves*.

This jump-off-the-bandwagon mentality is one which the "best" at anything in life seem to practice. Life on the bandwagon is safe and secure. Life off the wagon is an adventure for pathfinders only. I've always felt it would be better to jump off and die from the fall than never to have jumped at all! You simply cannot fly unless you get off your *perch*.

Recently, a twenty-three-year-old college graduate asked me for advice on his life's career and opportunities. I told him I don't give other people advice on how to lead their lives. However, I shared some thoughts with him. To help him visualize my suggestions, I used a blackboard and chalk. On the board I drew an X, and to the right a line two-feet long. I explained the X represented where he was at present—the horizontal line stood for time. At the end of the time line, I wrote the words, *mission/vision*.

I reminded him, "Young man, right now you're with a very good company. Why not consider staying there three to five years. During that time, ask a lot of questions, listen well, and do *more* than is expected of you. Understand *you* control your life; the company doesn't. When you're 27 or 28 years old, step back and review with your wife your *mission* and your *vision* of the future. Write down what you both want your life's menu to include in four or five years. Do you want money, free time, a big car, travel, adventure, peace and quiet, life in the fast lane, or life on a country road? Then draw a road map to your destination. It may mean leaving your current employer or you may achieve your three- to five-year goals and be perfectly happy staying where you are."

The key is not to believe anyone will *take care of you*. I've watched too many people put blind faith in someone in the business world only to see them die, get fired, or they discover their mentor is more interested in his or her own personal advancement.

To become who you are demands great inner strength and belief. It requires planning—taking control of your life. Be different. Break the mold—do your own thing. Everyone excels at something. Define what your *something* is and play hard to that strength.

Don't let anyone discourage you. Turn your strengths into a service others want and need. Then you're in business. If you help others in a specific area better than anyone else, you will have a lot of fun and make a good living to boot. Have the courage to become who you really are . . . and be prepared for great things to happen!

JUST NOTES

_____

_____

_____

_____

_____

_____

_____

_____

_____

"Accept everything about yourself—I mean everything. You are you and that is the beginning and the end—no apologies, no regrets."

Clark Moustakas

_____

_____

_____

_____

_____

_____

_____

_____

_____

_____

_____

_____

_____

Blue-Haired Ladies

It was obvious my client was impressed when I told him I'd made dinner reservations at one of Atlanta's finest restaurants. He exclaimed he'd never been there but had always wanted to go.

Upon arriving, we were greeted as if we owned the place and were escorted to our table overlooking the city skyline. The atmosphere was conducive to a relaxing evening. My colleague and I enjoyed a light drink as the pianist played some of my favorites from the '40s.

After 30 minutes or so my companion queried, "Joe, do you know where the men's room is?"

"Yes, just past the baby grand and up the stairs." Having dined there several years earlier, I remembered. He excused himself and returned shortly to continue our conversation.

Not long after he returned, I too had to visit the "cool chamber." I walked past the baby grand piano and up the stairs. Sure enough, there was the restroom door . . . I walked in. Now, let me tell you something. I've been in some nice restrooms in my time. Until this visit, one of the nicest had been in the Wrigley Building in Chicago. This Atlanta restroom, however, was beyond belief!

Gold-plated everything. Cherry-wood booths, marble all over the place. It was so beautiful, I felt this should not be a restroom but a REST room where one could relax and engage in pleasant conversation with friends. I went into one of the cherry-wood booths and soon was ready to exit through the beautiful polished door to wash my hands.

As I opened the door and stepped out onto the marble floor, there stood two little blue-haired ladies, dressed fit to kill complete with their diamond necklaces. I stared at them. They returned my stare. My mouth sagged open. Their mouths followed suit—one of them exclaimed, "Young man, what are you doing in here?"

"My God," I gasped. "I'm in the ladies' room!" and scurried out. I quickly found the men's room to retreat from reality. It looked more like the men's room I had expected to see earlier, if you know what I mean.

After washing my hands and face—and composing myself—I *slithered* down the stairs past the piano, and back to my friend.

"Where have you been?"

"In the ladies room," I admitted sheepishly. As I told the whole story, he burst out laughing.

As he tried to contain his mirth, I looked up and saw one of the blue-haired ladies approaching our table. I tried to crawl inside my skin as she drew near. Taking my hand, she consoled, "Young man, we all make mistakes. Please know that I understand you made a simple mistake. My friend and I could tell by the expression on your face that you had no intention of harming us."

"Boy what a compliment," I thought. Thank goodness this lady was not going to press charges or have us escorted out of the establishment.

Actually these ladies are very wise; they understand *anyone can make a simple mistake*—with no harm intended. And that's okay as long as we learn from our mistake.

I haven't been back to that restaurant since, but as Douglas McArthur said, "I shall return," hopefully to find the throne behind door number two!

JUST NOTES

_____

_____

_____

_____

_____

_____

_____

"Happiness? A good cigar, a good meal, and a good [wise] woman—or a bad woman. It depends on how much happiness you can handle."

George Burns

_____

_____

_____

_____

_____

_____

_____

_____

_____

_____

Do You Look
At Incidents or Trends?

Dagwood Bumstead has nothing on me. Briefcase in hand and dressed in my suit and tie, I was running late. I hit the door leading to my garage and bolted for my car only to have my belt loop catch on the latch of the screen door. It jerked me to a standstill. Unhooking myself from the door, I jumped in my car and sped off to work.

What I just described has happened to me several times over the years. This "incident" was just that—an *incident*. I went on about my business—a trend—and accomplished a great deal before returning home.

In the business world we get hung up on incidents and totally lose sight of the *trends*—good or bad. What if I had stopped when my pants were hung on the screen door and focused on that small incident all day? What if I had not gone on to work?

Often we have the tendency to let an *incident* ruin our day, failing to look down from a higher level and observe the *trend* of the day. Leaders focus on trends. When things go right at work and then one thing goes wrong, it is essential the leader not lose sight of the *trend*. The next time life slaps you down (professionally or personally) remember—this is only an incident, not a trend.

The same can be said of civilization. The *trend* for humankind today is the best it's ever been. If you don't believe me, check your history books and you'll soon discover the present trend is extremely positive.

A *smart* person may remember all the incidents in great detail. A *wise* leader focuses on the trends. Only then can positive directive leadership be offered to those who follow!

JUST NOTES

"We need people who influence their peers and who cannot be detoured from their convictions by peers who do not have the courage to have any convictions."

Joe Paterno

Listen to Me!

The manager had a puzzled look on his face when I asked him how his location was coming along on their continuous improvement process.

"Joe, we're showing substantial savings and I'm very pleased, but I need your help on something.

"Sure," I responded, "How can I help you?"

"Well, we're stumped on how to properly recognize our people. We've given hats, T-shirts, jackets, meals, movie tickets, and even a day off now and then. But it doesn't seem to satisfy many of our employees."

I asked if I could spend a couple of days on all four shifts and see if perhaps I could ascertain what might help. The manager eagerly agreed to permit me to conduct my informal survey.

The first place I visited was the cafeteria where employees ate breakfast, lunch, or dinner. I never cease to be amazed at what people will tell you if you *listen*. Next I stopped by the office areas, the factory floor, and the warehouse. Then I called on the security guards and the maintenance men outside. And so it went for two long days. I did not ask about *recognition*, but instead, I simply *listened* to whatever the people wanted to talk about. I asked some open-ended questions, such as, "Tell me about your continuous improvement process." As usual, the comments proved to be exciting and thought provoking, as well as humorous.

After two days of visiting and listening, my mind flashed back to a conversation I'd had with the president of a large corporation which had won the prestigious Malcolm Baldrige Award. He'd been on a fact-finding trip to Japan for several weeks with a number of other executives. Their purpose was to learn all they could about what Japanese managers do better than American managers. I had asked him what he learned in Japan that he didn't already know before he went.

He had replied, "That's easy. The Japanese do a much better job of listening to their employees than we do. Japanese management really believes the employees know the best answers to the problems they face, and they act accordingly. That's what I learned."

I was somewhat shocked and replied, "Surely you learned more than that!"

"No," he said. "That is exactly what I learned. Until American managers learn to *really* listen to our people, we will never catch up with Japan."

Reflecting on this conversation, I prepared to meet with my puzzled manager client in his office to report on my two days' visit with his people.

"Well, Joe, what did you learn?"

"You and your managers don't listen well." He turned a little red around the gills. I explained the very best form of recognition anyone can give is to listen with respect—then act on what is heard. All the T-shirts, hats, and meals in the world will not take the place of a boss who listens to, cares about, and respects his or her fellow associates.

Apparently my comments hit home. He called his staff together and to my amazement told them he knew he had not been listening to them and his behavior was going to change. He also challenged them to do what I had done—and to get cracking.

Some simple lessons must be learned over and over in the business world. *Hearing* is a physical exercise while *listening* is mental, requiring a great deal of concentration. How about you? Do you truly listen to your associates or do you just go through the motions?

JUST NOTES

_____

_____

_____

_____

_____

_____

_____

_____

"You will suddenly realize that the reason you never changed before was because you didn't want to."

Robert Schuller

_____

_____

_____

_____

_____

_____

_____

_____

_____

_____

_____

_____

_____

_____

The Wind Beneath His What?

The tall, well-groomed executive stood outside the Waldorf-Astoria Hotel in New York City, waiting for his limo. I was standing next to him, waiting as well . . . for a cab.

Two younger men, dressed fit to kill (as we say down south) were traveling with the tall gentleman. It was beginning to rain and the boss barked, "Umbrella!" His lieutenants immediately popped a huge parachute-sized parasol over his head.

"*Now, that's service,*" I thought to myself.

Smiling as his limo arrived, he got in, closed the door, and sped off—leaving his two associates standing there with me. By coincidence, we were all going to the Empire State Building. We chatted a moment, then all piled into a taxi the doorman flagged for us. In the car it was obvious these two men, in their mid thirties, were not eager to be with *the boss* again.

I couldn't resist. I asked, "Do you enjoy working for your boss?"

Looking at each other, one smiled, winked, and said with mock seriousness, "Oh, yes. We're the wind beneath his armpits."

All of us, cabby included, burst out laughing. Every time I hear that beautiful Bette Midler song on the radio now, I think of the strangest things!

JUST NOTES

_____

_____

_____

_____

_____

_____

_____

_____

"Beware, so long as you live, of judging men by their outward appearance."

La Fontaine

_____

_____

_____

_____

_____

_____

_____

_____

_____

_____

_____

_____

_____

_____

The Chimes

There is a lovely garden in Augusta, Georgia, which Kathy and I—at the invitation of two dear friends—visit every April. This particular garden is unique, you see, for the game of golf is played here.

Each spring, the masters of the golfing world gather to play at the Augusta National Golf Course. What has become known as "The Masters" has evolved over the years into an international event steeped in southern tradition. Few other sporting events can rival the excitement and beauty of this place which God and man have created together.

During the 1992 Saturday round of play, we found ourselves standing next to the fourth tee box just as Ian Woosnam, the defending Masters champion, prepared to tee off. The reverence paid to golf's elite is extraordinary in Augusta as thousands of people in the galleries quietly part to allow their heroes to walk uninterrupted from tee to green. This respect is evidenced as one stands among hundreds of other fans to hear only the song of a bird or the wind blowing through the tall Georgia pines. This quiet reverence for the golfers has become yet another tradition of the Masters.

On this particular afternoon, something extraordinary occurred as we stood waiting for Ian to tee off. The sound of a single chime was heard. The golfers and the gallery of fans looked at each other, not knowing what to think. Then the leader board,

---

which posts the leaders' scores, showed this message: "Storm warning." The chimes were now ringing in earnest as some 25,000 people scurried for cover.

A hidden public address system announced to all, "Take cover. Lightning has been reported in the area." Dark clouds moved in swiftly as the wind blew and lightning flashed all too close for comfort.

The leader board was completely cleared of all names and scores. Only two words showed on the entire board: "Play suspended." In an instant, everything had come to a complete halt. The world's golfing elite and their fans were all in the same situation. Lightning plays no favorites, whether you're a Masters champion or a duffer with a 30 handicap! For a brief time, golf did not matter—we were all equal at the Augusta National.

Chances are you too are a master at something. If not, you probably wouldn't be reading this book, hoping maybe to improve, to take one more stroke off your game. Regardless of how good you or I may be at what we do, the potential for lightning is always lurking. Life's storms can hit any of us, at any time, no matter what our skills or job titles, reducing us all to equals.

Illness, divorce, death, broken dreams—these harsh realities require understanding of what is and what is not important in life. Too often we look to the leader board and see our heroes' names, failing to realize they're no different than we are. They run from lightning too.

The next time you tee off at whatever you do best while others watch and perhaps envy you—try not to get too carried away with your success. Remember we're all in this together, and the chimes can and will sound without notice. Be ready for life's storms!

Joe Black

JUST NOTES

_____

_____

_____

_____

_____

_____

_____

_____

"I do not pray for success. I ask for faithfulness."

Mother Teresa

_____

_____

_____

_____

_____

_____

_____

_____

_____

_____

_____

_____

_____

_____

A Cry For Help

Do constantly ringing telephones drive you up the wall? At times, I've wished Alexander Graham Bell had never spoken those immortal words, "Watson, come here." With his analytical mind, he surely would have gone on to invent something else worthwhile had he not invented the telephone.

For some unknown reason, one day when my office phone rang, instead of hearing a loud ding-a-ling, I heard: "HELP! I NEED YOU. PLEASE ANSWER." Then I made the mental connection—every time my telephone rings, it is someone sending a code, a code that translates, "Help me. I need you."

Now doesn't that put a little different light on the subject of ringing phones? Almost without exception, a telephone call means an opportunity to help meet someone's needs or wants. Think about it that way the next time your phone cries, "Help!"

JUST NOTES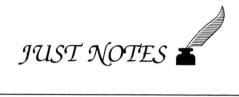

"The pessimist sees the difficulty in every opportunity; the optimist, the opportunity in every difficulty."

L. P. Jacks

Quality Roots

The shrubbery behind our home was ten years old. It was planted when the house was built. Some plants were growing out of control. The remaining ones looked pale and sickly. So I decided to do something about it.

Kathy and I researched the local landscapers' reputations for superior work and customer service. We reviewed several possibilities and decided to engage a firm from Columbus, North Carolina.

After surveying our yard and visiting with us, the landscape specialist presented a beautifully designed proposal for our back-yard. We walked over the areas to be improved, trying to visualize exactly where the berm would be and how attractive all new shrubbery would look. We became so excited with the idea we decided to add a winding brick walk from our patio past the dogwoods down to a grove of trees in the lower part of our yard. That's where my Pawley's Island rope hammock swings in the summer. I could just imagine myself taking that lovely walk from our patio to the hammock and snoozing in the shade of the Carolina pines.

Our landscaper expressed concern as I showed him the path I wanted the brick walk to follow. "Mr. Black, you run the risk of killing this pretty poplar tree if you put your walk here because we'll have to dig up a lot of roots."

I hadn't considered the many large, shallow roots in the path I chose. We certainly didn't want to kill the poplar tree. It provides generous shade over the patio during hot South Carolina summers.

Trees must have healthy roots to survive. Guess what? People need healthy roots too! People's roots are often described as friends, family, relationships with pets, good health, security, faith, careers, hope, love, etc. Reflecting on this, I asked myself, "Have I (knowingly or unknowingly) damaged someone's root system as I've made my path through life?" Isn't this a valid point for all of us to consider?

A person as well as a tree may die if the root system is damaged. Strong winds bend people as well as trees. Without strong roots, both people and trees can be uprooted and blown over. We need strong roots for the predictable storms, but we need especially deep ones when the unpredictable storms of life descend upon us. Our strong roots can help us bend but not break as adversity and change blow through our lives.

Think for a moment about your root system. If you're like me, you have some roots that run deep and others that are rather shallow. It's obvious we should depend more on deep roots in hard times. Our deepest are usually ones others can't see. Shallow roots often are the material things in our lives. But deep roots are usually intangible things that money can't buy— integrity, faith, hope, love, and strong personal relationships. Each of us would do well to make a list of our deep roots as well as reflecting on our shallow ones. Regardless of what forms they take, we humans—like our cousins the trees—must have a healthy system in order to survive and thrive.

It's wise to look around vigilantly as we go about building our paths and walkways through life. Let's be careful not to damage our own root systems or those of others. If we establish this root watching habit, we'll surely have a more enjoyable walk through life. Who knows—there may be some shade trees waiting for us with a hammock stretched between them as if to say, "Welcome, old friend. Thank you for caring. Please rest awhile!"

JUST NOTES

_____

_____

_____

_____

_____

_____

_____

_____

"Storms make oaks take deeper roots."

George Herbert

_____

_____

_____

_____

_____

_____

_____

_____

_____

_____

_____

_____

_____

My Wonderful
Hall of Love

Life is tough! I often hear people of all ages complain about just how rough life can be. I delight in saying, "Oh really, you mean you're already burned out at your age? I'm over 40 and not tired at all!"

Now I'll admit I get temporarily worn out, but you see I've got a secret. A source of fuel so powerful it will keep my engine running until I'm an old man.

Come with me . . . I'll let you in on it. . . .

"Good morning, Mr. Joe."
"Hi, Joe. How are you today?"
"Good to see you, Norman. Jennie."

"Oh, hi, Joe. How are you? I've missed you so."
"Liza, I'm fine. You're so sweet and pretty."

"How about it, Joe? Are we going to Trail's End this winter? You're not going to wimp out on us, are you? We're ready for Winterfest next February."
"Yes, Bob, Ben, Marett, Doug, Louis, Roy, Julien, Torrence, and Herb. I'll be there. Looking forward to it."

"Joe, I love you so. I enjoy being with you every day."
"I'm always with you too, Wellons. I love you, darling."

"Joe, do you think it will snow? Carrie's coming home for the weekend. Will you and Kathy come over if it snows? Maybe we can go sledding."

"Yes, Jud, we'll come over regardless. By the way, 'Dr. Joe' predicts 6-10 inches of snow by Saturday night."

"Hi, son, I hope you take care and don't work too hard. We love you."

"I love you too, Mama. Hi, Dad. Mama, come here and let me give you a big kiss."

"Hello, precious brother, I love you so. I'm very proud of you."

"Oh, Linda, I do love you! I'm fortunate to have you as my sister." (I kiss her picture.)

"My boy, I know you'll have a great day. I'm praying for you."

"Julia, my second mama. Thank you for loving me all the time."

"Hello, Señor Joe."

"Hello, Vince."

"I've been piddling around, doing some work for the church. They needed some bookshelves so I've been working on them."

"Vince, I love you. You're one in a million. Heard any good jokes lately?"

"Hi, Joe, it's grandmother."

"Yes, I know! Come here and I'll kiss you all over, you sweet thing."

"Oh, Joe, you do go on. I love you."

"I love you too, Gramps. I know you're always with me."

"Hello, Pamela and Roy. Let's trailer our horses to FENCE this Saturday and ride."

"Hey, Joe. Boy, I miss you."

"I miss you too, David. We had a good time on our trip, didn't we? Thanks for taking the time to talk to me each day."

"Hello, you beautiful Donna. You are one wonderful person. I admire you so."

"Tom and Marilyn. You two are so great. We'll see you in Colorado next month."

"Hey, Joe, when can we play some golf? Just call me. I'll work it in."

"Soon, Ben. I'll call. Tell Robin, Martin, and Phillip 'hello.'"

"Brett and I want to come see you folks. We're doing well and are planning a trip. Hope to see you and Kathy soon."

"Amy, you're great, honey. I'm so proud of you."

"Joe, I'm enjoying my job. I've got a new apartment."

"I'm proud of you, Heather. You have a wonderful day. I love you."

"Hello to all you grandparents and great aunts and uncles in heaven. Thanks for keeping in touch."

"We're always with you, Joe."

"I know. I can feel your wise counsel and energy, especially in difficult times. Thank you."

"Hi, honey. Ready for breakfast? You seem like you're in a good mood this morning."

"Yes, I am, Kathy. I just finished walking down our stairs and hallway. You know—my Hall of Love. I had a great visit with everybody."

All of the wonderful folks you've read about are represented by photographs hanging in *my* Hall of Love. I'm so blessed to have all this caring and support.

By the way, that's just the first floor. There are more on the second floor of our home. The miracle of love is everywhere if you just let it happen. Do you have a Hall of Love in your home? Are you connected to the people who love and support you? What a fantastic way to start the day!

JUST NOTES

"The world is so empty if one thinks only of mountains, rivers, and cities; but to know someone here and there who thinks and feels with us, and who, though distant, is close to us in spirit, this makes the earth an inhabited garden."

Goethe

Joe Black

Fit For Life

I would like to share with you a concern regarding ourselves and our nation. It has to do with being fit. "Fit for what?" you ask. Physically, mentally, and spiritually fit.

Being physically fit requires us to eat properly and exercise. Both dieting and exercising demand discipline and a certain degree of discomfort. Have you ever seen a weight lifter or a jogger smiling or singing? The expression on their faces leads us to believe they're about to drop. And have you ever heard a dieter talk about how much he or she's enjoying the new diet? I haven't.

Physical fitness has become a multi-billion dollar industry in the United States—dieting and exercising to enjoy life, live longer, look better, and stay younger longer. It's not only good for you, but the thing to do. We should all strive to get in shape and stay in shape for life's sake.

How about other kinds of fitness? Mental fitness, for instance. Being mentally fit requires us to *listen more* and *talk less*. We should ask good questions, read magazines, newspapers and books, avail ourselves of educational and training opportunities, etc.

How many books have you read this year? Like being physically fit, being mentally fit requires discipline and dedication. To remain mentally fit, we must become lifelong learners. We should never stop growing mentally.

Physically fit and mentally fit. Let's see—what about spiritual fitness? Being spiritually fit demands regular study and meditation. This usually requires great discipline and dedication. Spiritual fitness is the very core of our being. It's the essence of who we are.

Author Bernie Stiegel defines spirituality as "a state of mind that includes acceptance, faith, forgiveness, peace, and love."

Herb Miller writes that "spirituality is the *mental lens* through which we look at and interact with the reality around us, other people, and our future. That makes our spiritual makeup far more important than our psychological makeup, our sociological circumstances, or our cultural environment."

Spiritually fit people have great faith and are not anxious about tomorrow. The Greek word for anxious (*merimnao*) means "double-minded." Double-minded people are unstable, harassed, and haunted by what might happen or by something that has already happened—neither of which they can control or change.

Physical fitness, mental fitness and spiritual fitness—it would seem most folks put a lot more emphasis on one than the others. Reflect on your own life for a moment. Are you satisfied? Or do you need to concentrate more on a specific area?

Chances are if a person or a nation is not balanced in all three, they're not likely to be fit for the challenges and opportunities life offers. Fitness cannot be legislated—it must be *lived*!

JUST NOTES

_____

_____

_____

_____

_____

_____

_____

"The difference between ordinary and extraordinary people is that little extra."

Walter Paley

_____

_____

_____

_____

_____

_____

_____

_____

_____

_____

_____

_____

Just Gliding Along

In my travels I fly from city to city. I spend a good percentage of my time in transit from one airport concourse to another. When time permits, I enjoy some exercise by walking versus taking a train or the moving walkway. It seems travelers who appear to be physically fit usually are walking rather than taking the *easy way* provided by modern technology.

One day I decided to conduct a survey at Hartsfield International Airport in Atlanta by watching who uses the moving walkway. I stood in one location for 30 minutes logging the *fit* versus *fat* gliders. I computed the data in my unscientific poll. A whopping 76% of the people I observed standing on the moving walkway were overweight. The majority of these *gliders* were kids, teenagers, young adults, and middle-aged people. To my surprise, most of the older travelers were walking. The saying, "If you don't use it, you'll lose it," appears to be true.

Today's world affords each of us many choices. We can take the easy way requiring little or no discipline, work, or motivation and likely will lose "it." (You define the *it*.) We can choose the short-term glide mentality or the character-building and success-focused long-term walking mentality.

In your life today, are you Gliding or Walking:

In your educational life?

In your personal life?

In your physical life?

In your professional life?

In your spiritual life?

In your mental life?

In the final analysis, there aren't many short cuts to growing a well-rounded life. Building your life on a glide mentality is akin to building your home on a foundation of sand.

Are most of the people you know gliding or walking through life? Think about it. Isn't it wonderful we can choose to walk? If you're on a glider, let me urge you to get off. You'll be surprised how good it feels to walk again!

JUST NOTES

_____

_____

_____

_____

_____

_____

_____

"No pain, no gain; no thorns, no throne; no gall, no glory; no cross, no crown."

Penn

_____

_____

_____

_____

_____

_____

_____

_____

_____

_____

_____

_____

_____

Your Kitchen Table

After spending all my adult life in the corporate world, I've arrived at one abiding conclusion:

> The quality of what goes on around your family's kitchen table is far more important than . . .

> The quality of what goes on around your boardroom table.

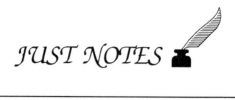

JUST NOTES

"Sometimes you just have to call a spade a damn shovel."

Marion R. Gramling

Farming For Quality

My Troybilt garden tiller roars to life each spring. For some 11 years, Kathy and I have enjoyed a vegetable garden in our backyard. Those juicy tomatoes, sweet corn, crunchy cucumbers, and fresh squash and peppers contribute to many an outstanding summer meal.

Throughout the country, millions of mini-farmers follow similar rituals of planting and harvesting. They have faith! Faith is a must if we are to be productive and successful gardeners. In farming as in life, the ground must be properly prepared before the crop can grow and produce. Preparing the soil, planting seeds or setting plants, watering, weeding, fertilizing, and pruning—all are essential to grow the best.

Of course, we could choose to go to a local supermarket and purchase our vegetables, wrapped in cellophane, off the shelf. They wouldn't taste as good—all kinds of chemicals on 'em— but no work's involved. *Easy* vegetables don't taste as good and are not as good for you as *earned* vegetables.

In today's business world, we see far more shoppers than farmers. The quick fix, off-the-shelf products come and go about as fast as seasons. Most managers love to shop. New fads, slogans, or management techniques to empower the masses are guaranteed to help heartburn and remove your corns and bunions. Well-meaning and not so well-meaning marketing experts sell these wares. Our country is overflowing with them.

Wait, folks. Stop. If you're committed to continuous improvement, better not go shopping. Learn to farm. Plant and grow a continuous improvement process for your company that is designed to fit your appetite. One that will last you a lifetime. That's plain old hard work and only *farming* will get you there. The next time some quality expert advises some quick-grown produce, you'd better check the shelf life before you buy. Hook up with a group that doesn't claim to have all the answers, but is willing to plow *your* field until they are uncovered.

I wish you joyful farming. Plant those rows long and straight now, you hear?

JUST NOTES

"Opportunity is missed by most people because it is dressed in overalls and looks like work."

Thomas Edison

The Five Steps
to Commitment

Ask any manager if he or she is committed to continuous improvement on the job and you're almost certain to get an affirmative response. When asked this question, no thinking person will respond negatively.

Then why is it so many people in responsible positions seem not to practice what they preach when it comes to quality and service? Why are you so often treated shabbily at your doctor's or dentist's office, gas station, auto repair shop, retail store, restaurant, or hotel?

Today, perhaps more than ever, America needs *leaders* in every walk of life who are committed to excellence in everything they do—people who dare to do the right things for the right reasons.

Why is it that cries for commitment, to this cause or another, so often appear to fall on deaf ears? Why do so many causes that seem noble and right at their inception fail in their implementation? The answer to these questions could be simply that we do not yet *understand* the stair-steps leading to true commitment and excellence.

Let's take a look at these steps:

                                        COMMITMENT
                               TRUST
                        BELIEF
              KNOWLEDGE
INTEREST

STEP 1: INTEREST

Before you or I will really learn anything we must first become interested in it. Beethoven was interested in music, Hemingway in writing, Henry Aaron in hitting home runs, Abraham Lincoln in preserving the Union, Arnold Palmer in golf, and Bob Hope in laughter. If we're going to learn about something, we must first be very interested.

STEP 2: KNOWLEDGE

When we're interested in something, we want to learn more about it. We read, ask questions, listen, attend seminars, classes, and workshops—and do everything we can to focus on and gain more knowledge about the subject. This base of knowledge becomes the bricks and mortar, the firm foundation on which to build belief.

STEP 3: BELIEF

Knowledge is not power. *Applied* knowledge is power. Unless we *believe* this knowledge will help us accomplish our goals and put them into practice, it is useless.

People are usually fanatical in believing in something in their lives. It may be a belief in their spouse, children, religion, or a football team. Let's face it—you can tell if somebody believes. It can't be faked—people can easily spot a phony. When you believe in quality and excellence, you can't hide it. You're . . . somehow . . . different.

STEP 4: TRUST

Trust is fostered by belief and is the very best form of human motivation. It takes patience and practice, but when you trust people, you bring out the best in them. Trusting means defining the task to be accomplished, delegating clearly, and letting go. That's right, let go! If you follow up, it's a sign you don't really trust that person.

This is not only hard to do, it is one of the more difficult facts to get through hard management heads. To trust means you allow mistakes and support your team members when they fail. That's how good coaches grow their players and nurture them to excellence. In any relationship, if you don't have trust, you can't get commitment.

STEP 5: COMMITMENT

Once we've achieved trust we're ready for true commitment. In my consulting work I often see companies asking their associates to be committed to continuous improvement. As leaders, coaches, and players, we should know why we are asking for this commitment. Are we asking for the right reasons, which include the associates' personal and professional growth? Or are we asking simply to increase our bottom line and make more money?

If we're smart, we understand today's enlightened associates wish to be challenged and treated with respect. They want to be involved in decision-making and they need to be listened to and trusted. They yearn for leaders who truly believe in them, who know them, and who are interested in them both on and off the job.

When our associates begin to understand we're genuinely interested in them, that we really care about them, believe in them, and trust them—then they'll become committed.

This amazing and rewarding five-step process is the stairway to commitment.

The elevator approach doesn't work and there is no escalator, so why not take the stairs? There just ain't no other way to get there!

JUST NOTES

_____

_____

_____

_____

_____

_____

_____

_____

_____

"The quality of any man's life is a full measure of that man's personal commitment to excellence and to victory, regardless of what field he may be in."

Vince Lombardi

_____

_____

_____

_____

_____

_____

_____

_____

_____

_____

_____

Stay in Touch!

Call me . . . Fax me . . . Write me . . .

Joe Black

Joe Black
Executive Quality Management, Inc.
205 E. Henry St.
Spartanburg, SC 29306
Fax: 803-573-6085

PHONE: 803-573-5234

Give the Gift
of Improvement to Your
Colleagues and Friends!

ORDER FORM

YES, I want _____ copies of *Looking Back on the Future: Building a Quality Foundation* at $16.95 each, plus $3 shipping per book. (South Carolina residents please include 85¢ state sales tax.) Canadian orders must be accompanied by a postal money order in US funds. Allow 30 days for delivery.

_____ Check/money order enclosed
Charge my: ___ VISA ___ MasterCard

Name _____

Phone (_____) _____

Address _____

City/State/Zip _____

Card # _____ Expires _____

Signature _____

Check your leading bookstore
Or call your credit card order to: 1-800-348-9953

Please make your check payable and return to:

Life Vision Books
P.O. Box 98
Campobello, SC 29322